ANNE WILLAN'S
LOOK & COOK

Main Dish Vegetables

ANNE WILLAN'S
LOOK & COOK

Main Dish Vegetables

DORLING KINDERSLEY, INC.
NEW YORK

A DORLING KINDERSLEY BOOK

Created and Produced by
CARROLL & BROWN LIMITED
5 Lonsdale Road
London NW6 6RA

Editorial Director Jeni Wright
Editors Norma MacMillan
Stella Vayne
Sally Poole
Art Editor Vicky Zentner
Designers Lucy De Rosa
Lyndel Donaldson
Wendy Rogers
Mary Staples
Lisa Webb

First American Edition, 1992
10 9 8 7 6 5 4 3 2 1

Published in the United States by
Dorling Kindersley, Inc., 232 Madison Avenue
New York, New York 10016

Willan, Anne.
  Main dish vegetables / by Anne Willan. – 1st American ed.
    p.   cm. – (Look and cook)
  Includes index.
  ISBN 1-56458-098-9
    1. Cookery (Vegetables)   I. Title.   II. Series: Willan, Anne.
Look and cook.
TX801.W497   1992
641.6'5 – dc20
                                                        92-5972
                                                        CIP

Reproduced by Colourscan, Singapore
Printed and bound in Italy by A. Mondadori, Verona

CONTENTS

VEGETABLES
THE LOOK & COOK APPROACH

Welcome to **Main Dish Vegetables,** and the *Look & Cook* series. These volumes are designed to be the simplest, most informative cookbooks you'll ever own. They are the closest I can come to sharing my techniques for cooking my own favorite recipes without actually being with you in the kitchen looking over your shoulder.

EQUIPMENT

Equipment and ingredients often determine whether or not you can cook a particular dish, so *Look & Cook* illustrates everything you need at the beginning of each recipe. You'll see at a glance how long a recipe takes to cook, how many servings it makes, what the finished dish looks like, and how much preparation can be done ahead. When you start to cook, you'll find the preparation and cooking are organized into easy-to-follow steps. Each stage is color-coded and everything is shown in photographs with brief text to go with each step. You will never be in doubt about what it is you are doing, why you are doing it, or how it should look.

INGREDIENTS

🍽 SERVES 6-8   🥘 WORK TIME 45-50 MINUTES   🍲 COOKING TIME 25-35 MINUTES

I've also included helpful hints and ideas under "Anne Says." These may list an alternative ingredient or piece of equipment, or sometimes the reason for using a certain method is explained, or there is advice on mastering a particular technique. Similarly, if there is a crucial stage in a recipe when things can go wrong, I've included some warnings called "Take Care."

Many of the photographs are annotated to pinpoint why certain pieces of equipment work best, or how the food should look at that stage of cooking. Because presentation is so important, a picture of the finished dish and serving suggestions are at the end of each recipe.

Thanks to all this information, you can't go wrong. I'll be with you every step of the way. So please, come with me into the kitchen to look, cook, and create some delicious **Main Dish Vegetables.**

WHY VEGETABLES?

Fresh vegetables play a major role in the way we eat today. Modern health concerns have made the combination of high vitamin and low fat content a popular choice at almost every meal. But if that weren't enough, the flavor and sweetness of vegetables at their prime is enough reward to enjoy them as the foundation of a main course. Whether you choose them stuffed or stir-fried, in a quiche or a stew, you'll find vegetable-based meals to savor all year round.

RECIPE CHOICE

The wide range of recipes given here offers a vegetable-based dish for all occasions and seasons. Choose Three-Pepper Pizza with Cheese or Calzone for a casual supper, Stuffed Vegetable Trio with Walnut-Garlic Sauce for a more elegant dinner. Summer Frittata with Ratatouille makes a delicious light warm-weather meal, while Mixed Vegetable Curry or Pumpkin Stew can star as hearty entrées for colder months.

BREADS AND TARTS

Flemish Vegetable Tart: In this rustic tart, a rich brioche crust holds a generous filling of colorful julienne vegetables in a light custard. *Pissaladière:* The French version of pizza has a Mediterranean topping of onions, herbs, anchovies, olives, and cherry tomatoes. *Three-Pepper Pizza with Cheese:* Three colors of bell pepper, with herbs and mozzarella, make a striking display on pizza dough spiced with black pepper. *Three-Pepper Calzone with Cheese:* Bell pepper filling is wrapped in individual turnovers of pizza dough. *Mushroom and Artichoke Pizzas:* Sautéed mushrooms and artichokes moistened with fresh tomato sauce top these cocktail-size pizzas. *Broccoli and Mushroom Quiche:* No main dish vegetable book would be complete without a quiche, the savory tart from Alsace that has swept the world. *Zucchini and Mushroom Quiche:* Rounds of zucchini, slices of mushroom, and cheese custard are baked in a pastry crust. *Phyllo Pie with Spicy Kale and Sausage:* A savory combination of kale, onions, and sausage meat fills a package of flaky phyllo pastry. *Potato and Blue Cheese Phyllo Pie:* Thin potato slices layered with blue cheese, bacon, and shallots make a hearty filling for this phyllo pie.

SOUPS AND STEWS

Vegetable Couscous: Vegetable-packed version of the traditional North African dish has a highly flavored broth and skewers of grilled zucchini, bell pepper, and cherry tomatoes. *Vegetable and Lamb Couscous:* Herbed lamb cubes are added to the vegetable kebabs, to be served with broth on a bed of couscous. *Fish Couscous:* Chunks of monkfish, cooked in a vegetable broth, accompany the couscous. *Genoese Minestrone:* Fresh vegetable soup chock full of red and white kidney beans and macaroni, with a purée of tomato, garlic, and basil stirred in for a burst of fresh flavor. *Soupe au Pistou, Croûtes Gratinées:* French version of minestrone, finished with cheese-topped toasts. *Borscht with Piroshki:* The brilliant red beet and cabbage soup is served with little cabbage- and cheese-filled turnovers. *Rustic Borscht:* This version is made with shredded beef. *Pumpkin Stew:* Hearty mixture of squash, leeks, tomatoes, celery, turnips, and bacon is served in the pumpkin shell, with hot sage biscuits. *Pumpkin Stew with Onion Topping:* Fried onion rings and bacon add crunch to savory pumpkin stew. *Mixed Vegetable Curry:* Carrots, potatoes, cauliflower, green beans, and peas are cooked with a fragrant blend of Indian spices and coconut milk. *Winter Vegetable Curry:* Curry takes a seasonal turn with winter vegetables cooked in the curry spice mixture.

COLD MAIN DISHES

Mediterranean Vegetable Platter with Garlic Sauce: A stunning platter of cold cooked Provençal vegetables is presented with a zesty garlic-herb sauce. *Vegetable Salad with Tahini Dressing:* The same array of prepared vegetables is complemented by a Middle-Eastern dipping sauce made from tahini (sesame seed paste), garlic, and lemon juice.

Mosaic of Vegetables with Chicken Mousse: Multicolored layers of carrots, green beans, and spinach are held in a light chicken mousse in this terrine, served with piquant mustard sauce. *Mosaic of Vegetables with Cheese:* A rich cheese custard binds layers of colorful vegetables together, and a red bell pepper sauce is the accompaniment.

HOT MAIN DISHES

Stuffed Vegetable Trio with Walnut-Garlic Sauce: Sweet onions, zucchini, and ripe tomatoes, with bulghur and mushroom stuffing, are served with a pungent sauce. *Wild-Rice-Stuffed Vegetable Trio:* Nutty wild rice and herbs make the filling for this trio of vegetables. *Vegetable Trio with Carrot-Rice Stuffing:* Vegetables are vivid with grated carrot in white rice stuffing. *Cabbage with Chestnut and Pork Stuffing:* Cabbage leaves are shaped around an unusual chestnut stuffing to resemble a whole cabbage. *Baby Green Cabbages Stuffed with Pork:* Pairs of cabbage leaves are filled

with a meaty mixture, shaped into balls, and simmered, to serve with sour cream. *Gratin of Endives and Ham:* Braised endive is wrapped in ham and topped with béchamel sauce sprinkled with cheese – delicious! *Broccoli and Cauliflower Gratin:* This vegetarian gratin combines green and white florets in a cheese sauce. *Individual Gratins of Leek and Ham:* Pale green leeks are baked in individual gratins and decorated with leek julienne. *Artichokes Stuffed with Mushrooms and Olives:* Pungent stuffing fills globe artichokes, served with red bell pepper sauce. *Artichokes with Herb-Butter Sauce:* Globe artichokes act as containers for herb-butter sauce. *Oriental Deep-Fried Vegetables:* Tempura batter creates a crisp, feather-light coating for a selection of vegetables, served with ginger dipping sauce. *Fritto Misto:* Deep-fried vegetables go Italian with breadcrumb-coated mushrooms and mozzarella sticks accompanying other batter-fried ingredients. *Swiss Chard Crêpes with Three Cheeses:* Sautéed Swiss chard combines with cheese to fill crêpes, topped with white cream sauce. *Crêpes with Wild Mushrooms and Herbs:* Crêpes are rolled around a succulent filling of wild and cultivated mushrooms. *Cheese-Stuffed Green Bell Peppers:* This version of Mexican "chiles rellenos" stuffs green bell peppers with cheese and onions and serves them with fresh tomato salsa. *Corn-Stuffed Red Bell Peppers:* Sweet yellow corn and red bell peppers make a colorful presentation. *Stir-Fried Thai Vegetables:* Thai seasonings – lemon grass, fish sauce (nam pla), and oyster sauce – flavor crisp stir-fried vegetables. *Chinese Stir-Fried Vegetables:* A different assortment of Oriental vegetables is stir-fried in a Chinese-style sauce. *Eggplant Cannelloni:* Lightly cooked slices of eggplant are rolled around a cheese filling and fresh basil and baked in thick tomato sauce. *Eggplant Napoleons:* An imaginative variation of puff pastry napoleon is made with sliced eggplant layered with cheeses and basil. *Summer Frittata with Ratatouille:* Italian version of an omelet, cooked with a ratatouille of late summer vegetables. *Corn, Scallion, and Red Pepper Frittata:* Yellow corn, green scallions, and red bell peppers make an eye-catching combination.

EQUIPMENT

Given the wide range of vegetables and the different methods of preparing them, a variety of equipment is needed. Happily, only a few items are specialized, and in almost all cases just standard kitchen tools are required, such as a colander for draining.

A chef's knife is essential for slicing or chopping large vegetables, with a small knife used for small-to-medium vegetables. The acid in some vegetables will discolor a carbon steel blade, so you may prefer to use a stainless steel serrated knife or a regular blade with a high stainless content. All knives should be sharpened regularly and stored carefully to prevent dulling. The peeler you choose, whether with a fixed or swivel blade, is up to you. You can use a melon baller for hollowing vegetables for stuffing, although a teaspoon does the job well, too.

A rolling pin will be needed for some of the quiches and savory pies in the book. Quiche and tart pans are required, too; the pan for phyllo pie must have a removable bottom. (It is not advisable to change the size of the pan called for in a recipe because the pastry quantity given will be wrong.) The Mosaic of Vegetables is baked in a terrine mold with lid, and you will need a deep-fat fryer for the Oriental Deep-Fried Vegetables. A pizza stone and paddle come in handy when making pizza, but baking sheets are an excellent alternative. Use a wok for stir-fried vegetables or substitute a large frying pan. A small frying pan works well if you don't have a crêpe pan.

INGREDIENTS

Vegetables combine with a wide array of other ingredients. Fresh herbs such as thyme, tarragon, basil, sage, fresh coriander (cilantro), and the ubiquitous parsley are always complementary. Spices and seasonings for vegetables range from nutmeg, hot chili peppers, cayenne, allspice, cinnamon, ginger, cumin, and ground coriander to the more exotic turmeric, fenugreek, and lemon grass. The juice of a lemon brings out the best flavor in almost all vegetables as well as often preventing discoloration. Certain vegetables enhance the flavor of others: almost all will benefit from the addition of onion or shallot, garlic, or tomato.

Cheese makes a winning combination when added to vegetable dishes, whether as a rich filling or a golden topping. Béchamel sauce provides a smooth coating for many main course dishes. Nuts add crunch to a stir-fry, texture to stuffing, and flavor to sauces. Another popular partner is grains: rice, wild rice, and bulghur all form substantial stuffings for baked or braised vegetables. And don't forget butter and olive and nut oils for enhancing flavor when frying or sautéing.

TECHNIQUES

Vegetables are so varied that almost every one calls for a specific technique. Some, such as leeks and wild mushrooms, must be cleaned very thoroughly. Artichoke bottoms and whole globe artichokes need careful trimming for cooking. Another basic preparation technique well worth mastering is chopping vegetables, particularly onions, shallots, and garlic, because this is essential to almost all recipes in the book. You will learn as well to peel bell peppers, to dice potatoes and zucchini, to cut turnips in julienne strips, and to roll-cut carrots. Preparing vegetables for stuffing is illustrated for a variety of vegetables, including tomatoes, bell peppers, cabbage leaves, and artichokes, all using different methods.

Turning to cooking, you will see why some vegetables must be blanched and refreshed with cold water, and why some are sprinkled with salt to draw out excess or bitter juices. Boiling and sautéing vegetables to the correct point is clearly illustrated, as is baking and braising vegetables until they are perfectly tender. Coordinating the cooking times of many different vegetables when making soups and stews is explained, as are grilling and shallow- and deep-frying.

As with other volumes in this series, techniques for preparing ingredients other than vegetables are also illustrated in these vegetable recipes. For example, you will find how to prepare chicken stock, how to make coconut milk, and how to make a bouquet garni.

FLEMISH VEGETABLE TART

 SERVES 8　🥣 WORK TIME 50-55 MINUTES*　♨ BAKING TIME 40-45 MINUTES

EQUIPMENT

chef's knife

small knife

medium saucepan with lid

vegetable peeler

whisk

pastry scraper

12-inch fluted quiche dish**

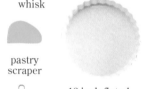

strainer

paper towels

rolling pin

plastic wrap

pastry brush

bowls

wooden spoon

chopping board

aluminum foil

**skillet can also be used

This hearty alternative to pizza uses brioche dough for the crust, with pretty strips of garden vegetables inside. A quick version of brioche is used here, to cut down on work time. For a rustic presentation, bake the tart in a skillet.

GETTING AHEAD

The brioche dough can be made and refrigerated overnight, but the tart is best eaten the day of baking.

* plus about 1½ hours rising time

SHOPPING LIST

For the brioche dough	
½ cake (9 g) compressed yeast, or 1½ tsp active dry yeast	
2 tbsp	lukewarm water
	vegetable oil for bowl
2 cups	flour, more if needed
1 tsp	salt
3	eggs
½ cup	unsalted butter, softened, more for dish and foil
For the vegetable filling	
1 lb	mushrooms
8-10	scallions
4	medium carrots
2	medium turnips
6 tbsp	unsalted butter
	salt and pepper
For the custard	
4	eggs
1 cup	heavy cream
¼ tsp	ground nutmeg

INGREDIENTS

compressed yeast

unsalted butter

flour

mushrooms

eggs

turnips

carrots

scallions

ground nutmeg

heavy cream

ORDER OF WORK

1 MAKE THE BRIOCHE DOUGH

2 PREPARE THE VEGETABLES

3 LINE THE QUICHE DISH

4 FILL AND BAKE THE TART

1 MAKE THE BRIOCHE DOUGH

1 Crumble or sprinkle the yeast over the water in a small bowl and let stand, 5 minutes. Lightly oil a medium bowl.

2 Sift the flour onto a work surface with the salt. Make a well in the center and add the yeast mixture and eggs to the well.

Be sure sides of flour well are high enough to contain liquids

Add whole eggs all at once

3 With your fingertips, work the ingredients in the well until thoroughly mixed. Draw in the flour with the pastry scraper and work into the other ingredients with your fingertips to form a smooth dough; add more flour if it is very sticky.

4 Knead the dough on a floured work surface, lifting it up and throwing it down until it is very elastic and resembles chamois leather, about 10 minutes. Work in more flour as necessary, so that at the end of kneading the dough is slightly sticky but peels easily from the work surface.

5 Add the butter, and pinch and squeeze to mix it into the dough, then knead on the work surface until smooth again, 3-5 minutes.

ANNE SAYS
"Alternatively, the dough can be kneaded and the butter added using an electric mixer fitted with a dough hook."

6 Shape the dough into a ball and put it into the oiled bowl. Cover it with plastic wrap and refrigerate about 1 hour. Or, if more convenient, the dough can be left to rise overnight in the refrigerator.

2 PREPARE THE VEGETABLES

1 Wipe the mushrooms clean with a damp paper towel and trim the stems level with the caps.

2 Set each mushroom stem-side down on the chopping board and, with the chef's knife, cut each one, into thin vertical slices. Stack the mushroom slices, then cut them across into very thin strips.

3 Trim the root ends from the scallions and slice them into small pieces.

Guide knife with curled fingers

Hold 3 or 4 scallions together for slicing

4 Peel and trim the carrots and turnips, then cut them into julienne strips (see box, page 13).

5 Melt the butter in the saucepan. Add the carrot julienne strips and cook gently, stirring occasionally, about 5 minutes.

6 Add the mushroom strips and turnip julienne to the saucepan and season with salt and pepper.

HOW TO CUT VEGETABLES IN JULIENNE STRIPS

Vegetables cut in julienne strips the size of fine matchsticks are quick to prepare and cook. The principle is much the same for celery, carrots, turnips, zucchini – whatever your selection.

1 After peeling and trimming, cut long vegetables into pieces about 3 inches long.

2 For rounded vegetables, cut a thin strip from one side so that the vegetable can lie flat on the chopping board as you slice.

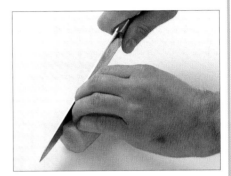

3 Holding the vegetable steady with one hand, cut it lengthwise into thin vertical slices.

Slice straight down to board

4 Stack the slices and cut into fine strips, keeping the tip of the knife on the board as you slice and guiding it with your curled fingers. Use a strip as a guide for length when cutting other vegetables.

7 Press a piece of buttered foil over the vegetables. Cover with the lid and cook until all the vegetables are tender, stirring occasionally, about 10 minutes longer.

! TAKE CARE !
The vegetables should steam gently in their own juices without browning.

Foil keeps steam around vegetables

8 Remove the saucepan from the heat, add the scallions, and stir to mix. Taste for seasoning.

3 LINE THE QUICHE DISH

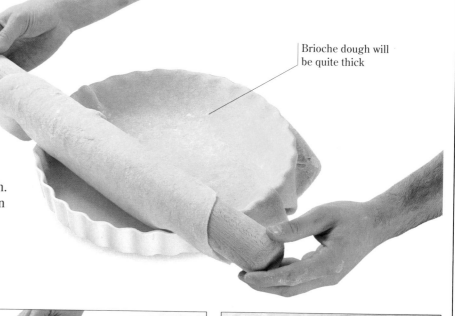

Brioche dough will be quite thick

1 Butter the quiche dish. Knead the brioche dough lightly to knock out the air. Lightly flour the work surface, then roll out the brioche dough to a round 3 inches larger than the dish. Roll the dough around the rolling pin and drape it over the dish.

! TAKE CARE !
Be careful not to stretch the dough.

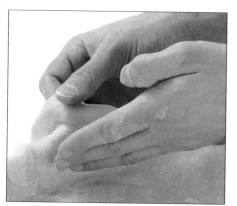

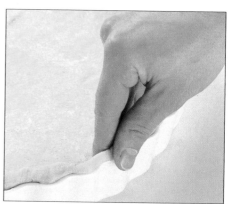

2 Gently lift the edges of the dough with one hand and press it well into the bottom and edge of the quiche dish with the other hand.

3 Roll the rolling pin over the top of the dish, pressing down on the pin to cut off the excess dough.

4 With your forefinger and thumb, press the dough evenly up the side, from the bottom, to increase the height of the dough rim.

4 FILL AND BAKE THE TART

Vegetables and custard will not fill dough case completely

Pour custard to cover vegetables evenly

1 Heat the oven to 400° F. Spoon the vegetable mixture into the dough case and spread it out evenly.

2 Whisk together the eggs, heavy cream, salt, pepper, and nutmeg. Pour the custard mixture over the vegetables.

ANNE SAYS
"Season the custard mixture well."

Press dough rim gently
onto custard filling

3 Fold the top edge of the dough rim over the filling to form a border. Let rise in a warm place until the dough is puffed, 20-30 minutes.

4 Bake in the heated oven until the brioche case is very brown and the custard is set when tested with the small knife, 40-45 minutes. If the top gets too brown, cover it with foil.

🍴 **TO SERVE**
Serve the tart hot or at room temperature.

Vegetable filling is rich and creamy

Golden crust is quick brioche dough

VARIATION

PISSALADIERE

1 Make the dough as directed.
2 Soak 2 ½ oz canned anchovy fillets in ½ cup milk, about 1 hour, then drain and cut the fillets lengthwise in half. Pit 1 cup black olives.
3 Peel 12 medium onions (total weight about 3 lb), leaving a little of the root attached; cut in half, then slice thinly.
4 Strip the leaves from a few sprigs each of fresh thyme and rosemary, pile them on the chopping board, and chop.
5 Heat ¼ cup olive oil in a large frying pan, add the onions, salt, and pepper. Cook until very soft, 25-30 minutes, stirring occasionally. Stir in the herbs.
6 Cut 1 cup cherry tomatoes in half.
7 Line the quiche dish with the brioche dough as directed, rolling the dough only 1 inch larger than the dish. Spread the onions on the bottom.

8 Make a diagonal lattice of anchovy fillets on top of the onions. Arrange the cherry tomato halves, cut-side up, and the black olives, decoratively on top. Let the tart rise as directed and bake until brown, 40-45 minutes.
9 Brush the top with a little olive oil before serving.

THREE-PEPPER PIZZA WITH CHEESE

 SERVES 4-6   WORK TIME 40-45 MINUTES*   BAKING TIME 20-25 MINUTES

EQUIPMENT

strainer

pastry scraper   frying pan

large metal spoon   small knife

chef's knife

pastry brush

slotted spoon

rolling pin

plastic wrap

bowls

chopping board   baking sheets**

** pizza paddle and pizza stone can also be used

Ever-popular pizza comes in many shapes and sizes. Here, three colors of bell peppers topped with mozzarella cheese form a striking display. The pizza dough is made with ground black pepper for a spicy flavor. Bell peppers should be brightly colored and firm, with no soft spots.

* plus 1 hour standing time

SHOPPING LIST

	For the pizza dough
1½ tsp	active dry yeast or ½ cake (9g) compressed yeast
1 cup	lukewarm water
3 cups	flour, more if needed
½ tsp	ground black pepper
	salt
2 tbsp	olive oil, more for bowl
	For the topping
2	medium red bell peppers
1	medium green bell pepper
1	medium yellow bell pepper
2	onions
1	small bunch of any fresh herb such as rosemary, thyme, basil, or parsley, or a mixture
3	garlic cloves
¼ cup	olive oil
	cayenne
6 oz	mozzarella cheese

INGREDIENTS

red, green, and yellow bell peppers

mozzarella cheese   cayenne

flour

garlic cloves   active dry yeast

onions

fresh herbs   olive oil

ANNE SAYS
"When shopping for fresh herbs, look for healthy sprigs that have a strong fragrance. Avoid bouquets with dried ends, discolored leaves, or wilted stalks."

ORDER OF WORK

1 MAKE THE PIZZA DOUGH

2 PREPARE THE TOPPING

3 ASSEMBLE AND BAKE THE PIZZA

1 MAKE THE PIZZA DOUGH

Pastry scraper draws flour in easily

1 Sprinkle or crumble the yeast over 2-3 tbsp of the water and let stand until dissolved, about 5 minutes. Lightly oil a large bowl.

2 Sift the flour onto a work surface with the ground black pepper and ¼ teaspoon salt. Make a well in the center and add the yeast mixture with the remaining water and the olive oil. Work the ingredients in the well with your fingertips, until thoroughly mixed.

3 Draw in the flour with the pastry scraper and work the flour into the other ingredients with your fingertips to form a smooth dough; add more flour if the dough is very sticky.

HOW TO CORE AND SEED BELL PEPPERS, AND CUT THEM INTO STRIPS OR DICE

The cores and seeds of bell peppers must always be discarded.

1 With a small knife, cut around each pepper core. Twist the cores and then carefully pull them out. Halve the peppers lengthwise and scrape out the seeds. Cut away the white ribs on the inside of the peppers.

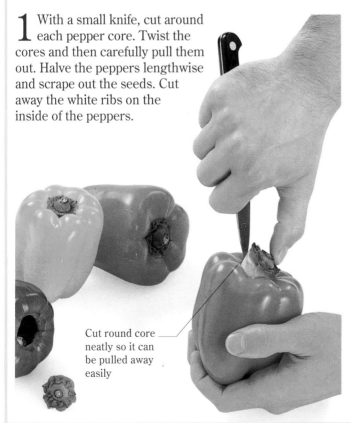

Cut round core neatly so it can be pulled away easily

2 Set each pepper half cut-side down on the work surface and press down on the top of the pepper half, with the heel of your hand, to flatten it for easier slicing.

3 With a chef's knife, slice each pepper half lengthwise into strips. For dice, gather the strips together in a pile and cut across.

4 Holding one end of the dough with one hand, press firmly down into the dough with the heel of your other hand, pushing away from you. Peel it back from the work surface in one piece, shape into a loose ball, and turn 90 degrees. Continue kneading until it is smooth and elastic, 5-8 minutes.

ANNE SAYS
"A good alternative to mixing and kneading the pizza dough by hand is to use an electric mixer which has been fitted with a dough hook."

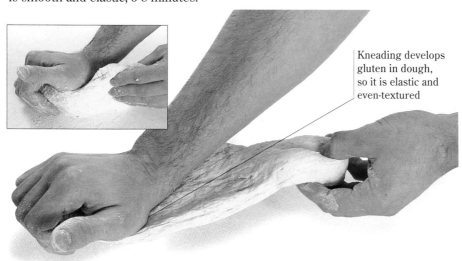

Kneading develops gluten in dough, so it is elastic and even-textured

5 Transfer the dough to the oiled bowl, cover it with plastic wrap, and let rise in a warm place until doubled in bulk, about 1 hour.

ANNE SAYS
"The dough can be left to rise overnight in the refrigerator, and it is easier to handle when chilled."

2 PREPARE THE TOPPING

1 Core and seed the red, green, and yellow bell peppers and cut them into strips (see box, page 17).

Brightly colored pepper halves should be sliced thinly for quick cooking

Use bent fingers to guide knife

2 Peel the onions, leaving a little of the root attached, and cut them in half through root and stem. Lay each onion half flat on the chopping board and cut vertically into thin slices.

ANNE SAYS
"The root holds the onion together."

3 Strip the herb leaves from the sprigs, pile on the chopping board, and finely chop. Finely chop the garlic (see box, page 20)

4 Heat 1 tbsp of the oil in the frying pan, add the onions, and cook, stirring, until soft but not brown, 2-3 minutes. Transfer to a bowl and set aside.

5 Add the remaining oil to the pan, then the peppers, garlic, and half of the herbs. Season with salt and cayenne. Sauté, stirring, until the peppers are softened but not brown, 7-10 minutes. Taste for seasoning: The mixture should be quite spicy. Let cool. Slice the mozzarella.

3 ASSEMBLE AND BAKE THE PIZZA

1 Heat the oven to 450° F. Put a baking sheet near the bottom to heat. Generously flour another.

Dough will shrink as it is rolled, so treat it firmly

2 Knead the dough lightly to knock out the air, then shape into a ball. Lightly flour the work surface. Flatten the dough into a round with the rolling pin. Pull and slap it into a round ³⁄₈ inch thick.

3 Transfer the dough to the floured baking sheet. Press up the edge of the dough round with your fingertips to form a shallow rim.

4 Spread the onions and then the peppers on the pizza base, leaving a ³⁄₄-inch border. Spoon any remaining oil from the pan over the peppers and top with the mozzarella. Let stand in a warm place until the dough is puffed, 10-15 minutes.

Dough rim keeps in juices from filling

HOW TO PEEL AND CHOP GARLIC

The strength of garlic varies with its age and dryness; use more when it is very fresh.

1 To separate garlic cloves, crush a bulb with the heel of your hand. Or, pull a clove from the bulb with your fingers. To peel the clove, lightly crush it with the flat side of a chef's knife to loosen the skin.

2 Peel off the skin from the garlic clove with your fingers.

3 To crush the clove, set the flat side of a knife on top and strike firmly with your fist. Finely chop the garlic with the knife, moving the blade back and forth.

5 With a sharp jerking movement, slide the pizza onto the heated baking sheet. Bake in the heated oven until browned, 20-25 minutes.

ANNE SAYS
"Putting the pizza onto a hot baking sheet ensures that the pizza base will cook thoroughly."

Slip away tray with sharp jerk

⃝ TO SERVE
Sprinkle the pizza with the remaining herbs and cut it into slices.

Pepper topping is sweet and spicy

Mozzarella cheese adds richness to pizza

GETTING AHEAD
The pizza dough can be made and the peppers can be prepared up to 12 hours ahead and kept refrigerated. Assemble the pizza and bake it just before serving.

V A R I A T I O N

MUSHROOM AND ARTICHOKE PIZZAS

Sautéed mushrooms and artichokes, moistened with tomato sauce, form the topping for these 20 cocktail-size pizzas.

1 Make the pizza dough as directed, omitting the pepper.
2 Prepare 4 medium globe artichoke bottoms. Half-fill a pan with water, add salt, then the artichokes. Weigh them down with a heatproof plate, bring to a boil, and simmer until tender, 15-20 minutes. Drain the artichokes and let cool to tepid. Scoop out the chokes with a teaspoon and cut bottoms into wedges. Alternatively, you can use canned or frozen artichoke bottoms, to save time.
3 Peel, seed, and chop 1½ lb tomatoes. Peel and finely chop 1 large onion and 3 garlic cloves. Heat 3 tbsp olive oil in a frying pan, add the onion, and cook until soft but not brown, 3-4 minutes. Add the tomatoes, garlic, 3 tbsp tomato paste, 1 bouquet garni, a small pinch of sugar, salt, and pepper. Cover and cook over low heat 10 minutes. Uncover and cook, stirring occasionally, until sauce is thick, about 15 minutes. Taste for seasoning.
4 Grate 4 oz Gruyère cheese.
5 Wipe 4 oz mushrooms with a damp paper towel and trim the stems even with the caps. Set the mushrooms stem-side down and slice them.
6 Sauté the mushrooms and artichokes as for the bell peppers, with the garlic and herbs, using 2 tbsp olive oil.
7 Roll and pull out the dough to ¼-inch thickness and cut it into shapes using a 4-inch cookie cutter (a flower-shaped cutter was used for the photograph).
8 Spread an even layer of tomato sauce over each pizza base, arrange the artichoke hearts and mushrooms on top, and sprinkle with the grated Gruyère. Let rise and then bake 10-15 minutes.
9 Arrange on a serving platter; decorate with parsley sprigs.

V A R I A T I O N

THREE-PEPPER CALZONE WITH CHEESE

The pizza dough and filling are reassembled in the shape of a turnover in this recipe, which serves 4.

1 Make the pizza dough as directed.
2 Prepare the topping as directed, and mix the onions and bell pepper strips together.
3 Divide the dough into 4 equal pieces. Roll and pull each piece into a square about ⅜-inch thick.

4 Spoon the bell pepper mixture onto a diagonal half of each square, leaving a 1-inch border. Arrange the mozzarella slices on top of the bell pepper mixture.
5 Moisten the edge of each square with water and fold one corner over to meet the other, forming a triangle.
6 Pinch the edges together to seal them. Put the triangles on the floured baking sheet and let rise. Whisk 1 egg with ½ tsp salt and brush this glaze over the calzone, marking a lattice on the floured surface. Bake them until golden brown, 15-20 minutes.
7 Brush the top of each calzone with a little olive oil and serve at once, decorated with a bouquet of fresh herbs.

BROCCOLI AND MUSHROOM QUICHE

 SERVES 6-8   WORK TIME 45-50 MINUTES*   BAKING TIME 30-35 MINUTES

EQUIPMENT

frying pan

bowls

metal spoon

aluminum foil

pastry scraper

10-inch tart pan

cheese grater

dry beans or rice

small knife

fork

colander

chef's knife

wooden spoon

whisk

rolling pin

strainer

ladle

paper towels   large saucepan

metal skewer

Quiche, the savory pie from Alsace, has swept the world. This version features pieces of broccoli on a bed of sautéed mushrooms. Look for broccoli with firm stems that are not dried out.

* plus 45 minutes standing time

SHOPPING LIST

1-2	heads of broccoli, total weight about 1 lb
	salt and pepper
6 oz	mushrooms
2	garlic cloves
2 tbsp	butter
	ground nutmeg
	For the pie pastry dough
1²/₃ cups	flour
1	egg yolk
¹/₂ tsp	salt
3 tbsp	water, more if needed
7 tbsp	unsalted butter, more for quiche pan
	For the cheese custard
3	eggs
2	egg yolks
1¹/₂ cups	milk
1 cup	heavy cream
¹/₂ cup	grated Parmesan cheese
	ground nutmeg

INGREDIENTS

mushrooms

broccoli

ground nutmeg

flour

garlic cloves

grated Parmesan cheese

milk

eggs

butter

egg yolks

heavy cream

ORDER OF WORK

1   MAKE THE PIE PASTRY DOUGH

2   LINE THE PAN

3   BLIND BAKE THE PASTRY SHELL

4   COOK THE VEGETABLES

5   ASSEMBLE AND BAKE THE QUICHE

1 MAKE THE PIE PASTRY DOUGH

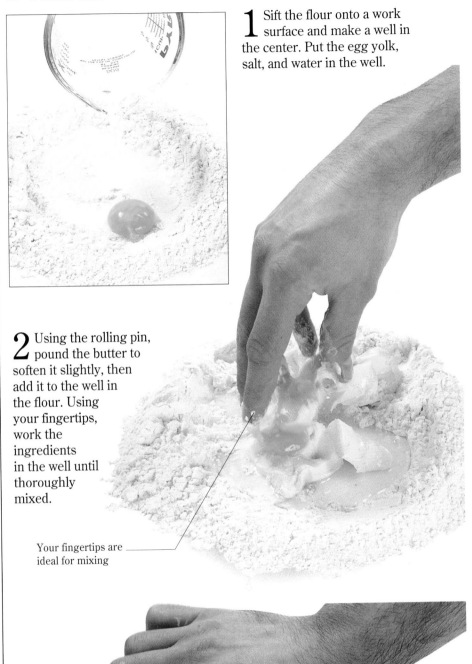

1 Sift the flour onto a work surface and make a well in the center. Put the egg yolk, salt, and water in the well.

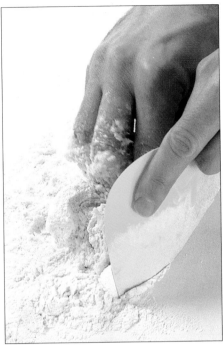

2 Using the rolling pin, pound the butter to soften it slightly, then add it to the well in the flour. Using your fingertips, work the ingredients in the well until thoroughly mixed.

Your fingertips are ideal for mixing

3 Draw in the flour with the pastry scraper. With your fingers, work the flour into the other ingredients until coarse crumbs form. Press the dough into a ball.

ANNE SAYS
"*If the dough is very dry, sprinkle it with more water.*"

Knead dough until it is very pliable

4 Lightly flour the work surface, then blend the dough by pushing it away from you with the heel of your hand. Gather it up with the pastry scraper and continue to blend until it is very smooth and peels away from the work surface in one piece, 1-2 minutes.

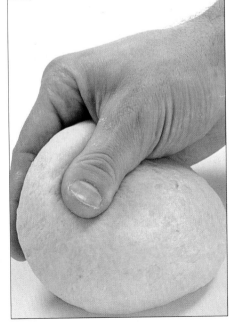

5 Shape the pastry dough into a ball, wrap it tightly, and chill until firm, about 30 minutes.

2 LINE THE PAN

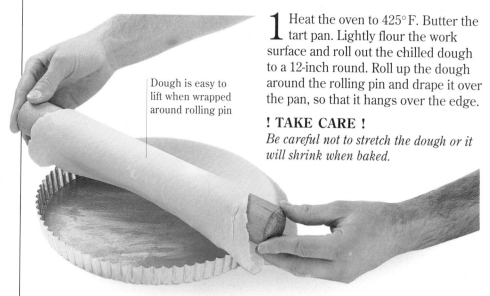

Dough is easy to lift when wrapped around rolling pin

1 Heat the oven to 425° F. Butter the tart pan. Lightly flour the work surface and roll out the chilled dough to a 12-inch round. Roll up the dough around the rolling pin and drape it over the pan, so that it hangs over the edge.

! TAKE CARE !
Be careful not to stretch the dough or it will shrink when baked.

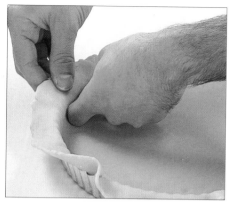

2 Gently lift the edge of the dough with one hand and press it well into the bottom edge of the pan with the forefinger of the other hand.

3 Roll the rolling pin over the top of the pan, pressing down on the pin to cut off the excess dough.

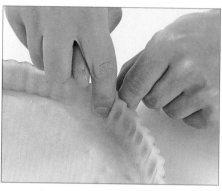

4 With your forefingers and thumb, press the dough evenly up the side, from the bottom, to increase the height of the dough rim.

5 Prick the bottom of the shell with the fork to prevent air bubbles from forming during baking. Chill until firm, at least 15 minutes.

3 BLIND BAKE THE PASTRY SHELL

1 Line the pastry dough shell with a double thickness of foil, pressing it well into the bottom edge. If necessary, trim the foil so it stands 1½ inches above the edge of the pan.

Foil supports dough so it does not lose shape in baking

2 Three-quarters-fill the foil with dry beans or rice to weigh down the dough while it is baking.

3 Bake the pastry dough shell until set and starting to brown, about 15 minutes. While the pastry shell is baking, cook the vegetables. Remove the foil and beans; reduce the oven heat to 375° F.

4 Continue baking until the pastry is lightly browned, about 5 minutes longer. Remove the pastry shell from the oven and test with your hand whether the pastry is set. Set aside; leave the oven on.

4 COOK THE VEGETABLES

1 Trim the head of broccoli, leaving about 2 inches of stem. With the small knife, strip the tough outer skin from the stem.

Drain broccoli as soon as it is tender

Use colander to drain broccoli thoroughly

2 Cut the florets from the stem where they begin to branch. Slice the stem lengthwise into sticks.

3 Half-fill the saucepan with water, and bring to a boil, add salt, then add the broccoli. Cook until just tender, 3-5 minutes. Drain, rinse with cold water, and drain again thoroughly.

HOW TO CLEAN AND SLICE MUSHROOMS

Mushrooms need to be cleaned carefully if they are dirty. Be sure to rinse them in water only 1-2 seconds; do not soak because they quickly become waterlogged.

1 Wipe the mushrooms clean with a damp paper towel or cloth. If they are very dirty, plunge into cold water, swirl around, and lift out to drain in a colander.

2 With a small knife, trim the stems just level with the caps. If using wild mushrooms, trim just the ends of the stems.

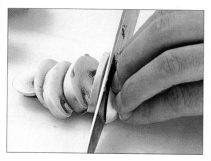

3 To slice, hold the mushrooms stem-side down on the chopping board and cut them vertically with a chef's knife into slices of the required thickness.

4 Clean and slice the mushrooms (see box, left). Set the flat side of the chef's knife on top of each garlic clove and strike it with your fist. Discard the skin and finely chop the garlic cloves.

5 Melt the butter in the frying pan. Add the mushrooms, garlic, salt, pepper, and a pinch of nutmeg. Cook, stirring, until the liquid has evaporated, about 5 minutes. Taste for seasoning.

! TAKE CARE !
Cook the mushrooms until quite dry or they may curdle the filling.

5 ASSEMBLE AND BAKE THE QUICHE

1 Make the cheese custard: Whisk the eggs, egg yolks, milk, cream, grated cheese, salt, pepper, and a pinch of nutmeg together in a small bowl.

2 Spread the sautéed mushrooms on the bottom of the pastry shell. Arrange the broccoli florets and sticks of broccoli stem on top in concentric circles.

Make neat pattern with broccoli in pastry shell

ZUCCHINI AND MUSHROOM QUICHE

Rounds of zucchini replace the broccoli in this quiche.

3 Ladle the cheese custard over the vegetables to fill the pastry shell almost to the rim.

Broccoli florets show temptingly through custard

4 Bake the quiche in the oven until browned and the cheese custard is set when tested with the metal skewer, 30-35 minutes.

ANNE SAYS
"The skewer inserted in the center of the quiche should come out clean."

TO SERVE
Cut the quiche into wedges and serve hot or at room temperature.

Parmesan-flavored custard holds tender pieces of broccoli and mushroom

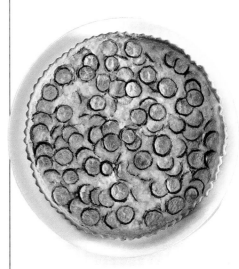

1 Make the pastry dough. Line and blind bake the pastry shell as directed.
2 Trim 3 medium zucchini (total weight about 12 oz) and cut them into thin slices. Half-fill a saucepan with water, bring to a boil. Add salt, and blanch the zucchini until just tender, 1-2 minutes. Drain, rinse with cold water, then pat dry with paper towels.
3 Cook the mushrooms and prepare the cheese custard as directed.
4 Assemble the quiche, arranging the zucchini slices attractively on top of the mushrooms. Pour the custard over the vegetables and bake as directed.

Pastry is crisp and buttery

GETTING AHEAD
The quiche can be made 2 days ahead and kept, tightly covered, in the refrigerator. However, the pastry tends to get soft, so reheat it in a 350° F oven for 10-15 minutes before serving.

PHYLLO PIE WITH SPICY KALE AND SAUSAGE

 SERVES 6 WORK TIME 35-40 MINUTES BAKING TIME 45-55 MINUTES

EQUIPMENT

chef's knife

wooden spoon

slotted spoon

fork

pastry brush

colander

kitchen scissors

bowls

sauté pan with lid*

small saucepan

chopping board

11-inch round loose-based tart pan

dish towels

*frying pan with lid can also be used

INGREDIENTS

kale

eggs

onions

butter

phyllo dough

sausage meat

ground allspice

ANNE SAYS
"For a vegetarian phyllo pie, the sausage meat can be omitted from the filling."

Based on the Greek spinach pie, "spanokopita," this recipe combines kale with onions, spice, and sausage meat inside a package of golden brown flaky phyllo pastry. Other hearty greens can be substituted for the kale in the filling: Mustard greens, collards, dandelion, or even spinach can be used instead. Choose young greens with small tender leaves, avoiding tough woody stems which show old age.

GETTING AHEAD

The pie can be prepared, wrapped securely, and kept in the refrigerator up to 2 days; it also freezes well. Bake just before serving.

SHOPPING LIST

³/₄ cup	butter
1 lb	package phyllo dough
	For the kale and sausage filling
1¹/₂ lb	kale
3	medium onions
8 oz	sausage meat
2 tbsp	butter
¹/₂ tsp	ground allspice
	salt and pepper
2	eggs

ORDER OF WORK

1. **PREPARE THE VEGETABLES FOR THE FILLING**

2. **COOK THE INGREDIENTS FOR THE FILLING**

3. **ASSEMBLE AND BAKE THE PIE**

1 PREPARE THE VEGETABLES FOR THE FILLING

Loosely rolling kale makes cutting easy

1 Using the colander, wash the kale thoroughly, then discard any thick stems. Take a few leaves of kale at a time, roll them up loosely, and cut across into thin strips. Chop the onions (see box, below).

HOW TO CHOP AN ONION

An onion can be sliced, then cut into even dice or chopped more finely if called for in a recipe. The size of the dice depends on the thickness of the initial slices. For a standard size, make slices that are about ¼ inch thick. For finely chopped onions, slice as thinly as possible.

1 Peel the onion and trim the top; leave a little of the root attached to hold the onion together.

2 Cut the onion lengthwise in half, through root and stem.

3 Put one half, cut-side down, on the chopping board and hold the onion steady with one hand. Using a chef's knife, make a series of horizontal cuts from the top toward the root (but not through it).

4 Make a series of lengthwise vertical cuts, cutting just to the root but not through it.

ANNE SAYS
"When slicing, tuck your fingertips under and use your knuckles to guide the blade of the knife."

5 Slice the onion crosswise into dice. For finely chopped onion, continue chopping until you have the fineness required.

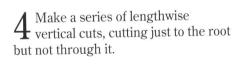

Neat dice are easily obtained this way

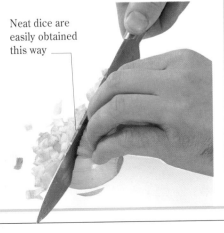

2 COOK THE INGREDIENTS FOR THE FILLING

1 If necessary, remove the sausage meat from its casings and crumble it. Heat the butter in the sauté pan, add the sausage, and cook, stirring, until it is crumbly and brown, 3-5 minutes.

Lightly fried sausage meat has crumbly texture

2 Transfer the sausage meat to a bowl with the slotted spoon, leaving the sausage fat behind.

Stir constantly with wooden spoon

3 Add the onions to the pan and cook, stirring, until soft.

ANNE SAYS
"You may have to add the kale in batches, adding more as each batch softens."

Kale retains vivid green color

4 Add the kale strips, then cover with the lid and cook very gently until the kale is wilted, 3-5 minutes. Remove the lid and cook, stirring constantly, until the moisture has evaporated, about 5 minutes.

Sausage meat adds richness to filling

5 Return the sausage meat to the pan with the allspice and stir into the kale mixture. Season to taste with salt and plenty of pepper. Remove from the heat and let cool completely.

6 Lightly beat the eggs with the fork and stir them into the filling.

3 ASSEMBLE AND BAKE THE PIE

1 Heat the oven to 350° F. Melt the butter in the saucepan; brush the tart pan with a little of the butter.

Work quickly with phyllo dough so it does not dry out

2 Lay a folded damp dish towel on the work surface. Unroll the phyllo dough sheets onto the towel.

3 Using the tart pan as a guide, cut through the pastry sheets to leave a 3-inch border around the pan where possible. Reserve the trimmings for garnish. Cover the sheets and trimmings with a second folded damp towel.

! TAKE CARE !
Do not let the phyllo dough dry out or it will be hard to work with.

Handle dough gently to avoid tearing it

4 Put 1 phyllo sheet on top of a third damp towel and brush the phyllo lightly with butter. Transfer the buttered sheet to the tart pan, pressing it well into the side.

A few creases in dough do not matter

5 Butter another phyllo sheet and put it in the pan at a right angle to the first. Continue buttering and layering until half of the phyllo is used, arranging each alternate layer at right angles.

Spoon in filling, still working quickly

6 Spoon the kale and sausage filling into the phyllo dough case and spread it out evenly over the bottom of the case with the back of the spoon.

7 Butter another sheet of phyllo dough and cover the filling with it. Top with the remaining sheets of phyllo, brushing each, including the top one, with melted butter.

8 Fold the overhanging dough up around the edge of the pie top, tucking it around your finger and pressing it around the pan edge, pinching with fingers and thumbs to form ridges.

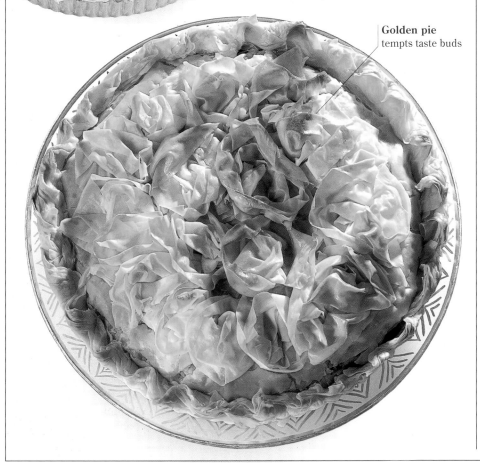

Deft touch will ensure dough adheres easily

9 Cut the phyllo dough trimmings into 2-inch-wide strips. Pleat them to form ruffles and arrange on top of the pie so it is completely covered. Drizzle the remaining melted butter over the top. Bake the pie in the heated oven until golden brown, 45-55 minutes. Let the pie cool slightly, then cut into wedges and serve hot or at room temperature.

! TAKE CARE !
If the pie browns too quickly, cover it with a piece of foil.

Golden pie tempts taste buds

V A R I A T I O N

POTATO AND BLUE CHEESE PHYLLO PIE

1 Peel 2 lb potatoes and cut into very thin slices. Cover with a damp towel.
2 Separate 4 shallots into sections, and peel each section. Using a small knife, slice each section horizontally toward the root, leaving the slices attached at the root. Slice vertically, again leaving the root end uncut, then cut across to make fine dice.
3 Strip the leaves from a few sprigs each of fresh parsley, tarragon, and chervil and pile them on the chopping board. With the chef's knife, finely chop the leaves.
4 Trim the rind from 4 oz blue cheese, then crumble it. Cut 4 oz bacon into strips. Heat 1 tbsp butter in a frying pan, add the bacon, and cook until brown, about 5 minutes. Transfer to paper towels to drain.
5 Trim the phyllo sheets and line the tart pan with half of the sheets as directed. Arrange half of the potatoes in an overlapping layer in the tart pan. Sprinkle with half of the blue cheese, bacon strips, chopped shallots, herbs, salt, and pepper. Repeat with the remaining potatoes, cheese, bacon, shallots, and herbs.
6 Cover the pie with the remaining phyllo sheets, buttering each one. Cut a 3-inch circle from the center of the dough lid using a cookie cutter or glass, so the filling shows through.
7 Finish the pie with the dough strips and bake as directed. While still hot, spoon 3-4 tbsp sour cream into the center of the pie and serve at once.

VEGETABLE COUSCOUS

 SERVES 8 WORK TIME 35-40 MINUTES* COOKING TIME 35-40 MINUTES

EQUIPMENT

16 bamboo skewers,
each 6-inches long**

wooden spoon

slotted spoon

large metal spoon

kitchen string   paper towels

fork

vegetable peeler   small knife

chef's knife

strainer   large shallow dish

bowls

colander

baking sheet   chopping
board

saucepans

**metal skewers can also be used

Couscous looks and cooks like a grain, though in fact it is made from a wheat-flour dough. Here it is served in Algerian style with an aromatic broth and broiled skewers of herbed vegetables.

* plus 1-2 hours marinating time

SHOPPING LIST

1 lb	couscous
2 cups	boiling water, more if needed
3-4 tbsp	butter
For the vegetable broth	
	saffron threads
3-4 tbsp	hot water
4 lb	mixed vegetables: 2 leeks, 2 zucchini, 2 carrots, 2 turnips, 1 onion, and 3 tomatoes
2 cups	canned chickpeas
2 tbsp	olive oil
2 quarts	chicken stock
1	bouquet garni
1 tsp each	ground ginger, turmeric and paprika
	salt and pepper
For the vegetable kebabs	
2	medium zucchini, total weight about 12 oz
2	large red bell peppers, total weight about 8 oz
8 oz	mushrooms
5-6	small onions, total weight about 12 oz
8 oz	cherry or medium tomatoes
1	small bunch of fresh coriander (cilantro)
4-6	sprigs of fresh thyme
½ cup	olive oil
1 tsp	ground cumin

INGREDIENTS

zucchini   bouquet garni

leeks

turnips

mushrooms   tomatoes

onions   carrots

red bell   fresh
peppers   coriander

chicken stock   fresh   chickpeas
thyme

saffron
threads

butter

couscous   ground   olive oil
spices

ORDER OF WORK

1 MAKE THE
VEGETABLE BROTH

2 PREPARE THE
VEGETABLE KEBABS

3 BROIL THE KEBABS
AND PREPARE THE
COUSCOUS

1 MAKE THE VEGETABLE BROTH

1 Put a large pinch of saffron threads in a small bowl and pour over the hot water. Set aside to steep. Cut the leeks into strips (see box, below).

Cut zucchini into sticks of equal size so they cook evenly

2 Trim the zucchini and cut them across into 3-inch lengths. Cut the pieces lengthwise into ½-inch slices, then stack the slices and cut into ½-inch sticks. Peel the carrots and turnips, square off the sides, and cut into sticks as for the zucchini.

3 Peel the onion, leaving a little of the root attached, and cut it in half through the root and stem. Slice each half horizontally toward the root, leaving the slices attached at the root end, then slice vertically. Finally, cut across the onion to make dice.

HOW TO PREPARE LEEKS AND CUT INTO STRIPS

1 Trim the leeks, discarding the root and the tough green tops. Slit them lengthwise and wash them thoroughly under cold running water in a colander.

2 Cut a leek half crosswise into 3-inch lengths, then cut each of the pieces lengthwise in half.

3 Fan each half lightly so that it lays flat on the chopping board and cut lengthwise into ½-inch strips. Repeat cutting and fanning with each remaining leek half.

4 Cut the cores from the tomatoes and score an "x" on the base of each with the tip of a knife. Immerse them in a pan of boiling water until the skin starts to split, 8-15 seconds depending on ripeness. Transfer them at once to a bowl of cold water. When cold, peel off the skin.

5 With the chef's knife, cut the tomatoes crosswise in half and squeeze out the seeds, then coarsely chop each half. Drain the canned chickpeas in the strainer and rinse them thoroughly with cold water.

6 Heat the oil in a large saucepan, add the onion, and cook, stirring with the wooden spoon, until soft but not brown, 2-3 minutes. Add the tomatoes and cook, stirring, until thickened, about 5 minutes.

7 Add the chicken stock to the onion and tomatoes with the zucchini, carrot, and turnip sticks, the leeks, bouquet garni, and chickpeas. Stir in the ginger, turmeric, paprika, saffron with its liquid, salt, and pepper.

Soaked saffron will give rich color and flavor to vegetable broth

Bouquet garni of fresh herbs is tied with string

8 Bring to a boil and simmer until the vegetables are just tender, 15-20 minutes. Discard the bouquet garni. Taste the broth for seasoning.

2 PREPARE THE VEGETABLE KEBABS

1 Trim the zucchini. Cut each one lengthwise into quarters, then across into 1½-inch pieces.

2 With a sharp movement, twist the cores out of the bell peppers, then halve the peppers and scrape out the seeds. Cut peppers into large squares.

3 Wipe the mushrooms with a damp paper towel; trim the stems level with the caps. Cut vertically in half, or into quarters if large.

4 Cut the onions into quarters, leaving on a little root to hold them together. Pick over the cherry tomatoes. Or, cut medium tomatoes into quarters, then cut the quarters crosswise in half.

Choose small onions to make vegetable skewers attractive

Herb and oil marinade gives delicious flavor to vegetables

5 Strip the coriander and thyme leaves from the stems and pile them on the chopping board. With the chef's knife, finely chop the leaves. Set aside 1-2 tbsp for sprinkling before serving; put the remainder in a small bowl and mix in the olive oil.

6 Put the mushrooms, zucchini, bell peppers, onions, and tomatoes in a large bowl. Pour the herb and olive oil mixture over the vegetables.

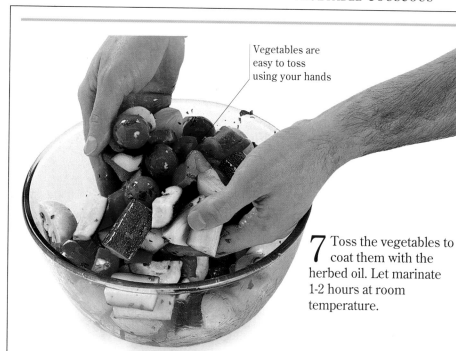

Vegetables are easy to toss using your hands

7 Toss the vegetables to coat them with the herbed oil. Let marinate 1-2 hours at room temperature.

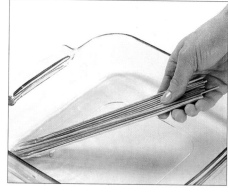

8 Meanwhile, immerse the bamboo skewers in water in the shallow dish and set aside to soak.

ANNE SAYS
"Soaking prevents bamboo skewers from burning when broiled."

3 BROIL THE KEBABS AND PREPARE THE COUSCOUS

2 Set the kebabs on the oiled baking sheet and broil them about 3 inches from the heat until browned, about 5 minutes. Turn the kebabs and broil on the other side until browned and tender, about 5 minutes longer.

Leave ends of skewers free so you can pick them up

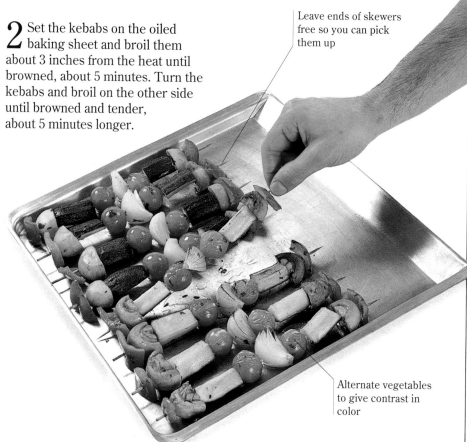

1 Heat the broiler. Take the soaked skewers from the water, and thread the vegetables onto them, alternating the bell pepper, mushroom, zucchini, tomatoes, and onion. Scrape any herbs from the bowl; brush on the kebabs.

Alternate vegetables to give contrast in color

3 While the kebabs are broiling, prepare the couscous: Put the couscous in a large bowl and pour the boiling water over it, stirring quickly with the fork. Let the couscous sit until plump, about 5 minutes.

ANNE SAYS
"The quantity of boiling water required may vary with the couscous you use, so check the package directions."

4 Add the butter, salt, and pepper to the couscous. Stir and toss with the fork to fluff the grains and incorporate the butter. Taste for seasoning.

🍽 TO SERVE

Reheat the vegetable broth if necessary and transfer it to a deep serving bowl. Pile the couscous on a warmed serving platter. Sprinkle the kebabs with salt, pepper, cumin, and the reserved chopped herbs. Arrange the skewers in the center of the couscous; serve with fiery harissa (Moroccan hot sauce).

Vegetable broth is warmly spiced

Vegetable kebabs are flavored with fresh herbs

1 Cut 2 lb monkfish fillets into even-sized 2-inch pieces.
2 Make the vegetable broth as directed, using water in place of the chicken stock and replacing the ground ginger with 1½ tsp ground cumin. After simmering 5-10 minutes, add the monkfish pieces and continue simmering gently until the fish is flaky and the vegetables are tender, 10-12 minutes longer.
3 Omit the vegetable kebabs, and prepare the couscous as directed.
4 Divide the couscous among warmed individual dishes. Put the hot broth into a well made in the center of each serving and arrange the fish around the edge. Decorate with parsley.

1 Bring a large pan of water to a boil and add 2 lb lamb or veal bones, cut into pieces. Return to a boil; simmer 5 minutes. Drain and rinse the bones.
2 Make the vegetable broth as directed, using water instead of chicken stock and adding the blanched bones with the water. Do not yet add the vegetable sticks, chickpeas, or spices. Simmer, skimming occasionally, 45-60 minutes.
3 Trim the fat from 1 lb boneless lamb shoulder; cut meat into 1-inch cubes.
4 Prepare the mushrooms, red bell peppers, and onions for the kebabs, omitting the zucchini and tomatoes. Add the lamb cubes with the herbs and oil. Toss and let marinate 1-2 hours.
5 Strain the broth. Add the vegetable sticks with the chickpeas and spices and continue cooking as directed.
6 Thread the red bell peppers, lamb cubes, onion, and mushroom onto the skewers and broil, 4-5 minutes per side. Sprinkle with the cumin, chopped chives, salt, and pepper.
7 Prepare the couscous as directed. Divide it among warmed individual shallow dishes. Put the hot vegetable broth into a well made in the center of each serving and the kebabs on top. Decorate with parsley.

GETTING AHEAD
The broth can be made up to 2 days in advance and kept, covered, in the refrigerator, or it can be frozen. The kebabs and couscous are best cooked just before serving.

GENOESE MINESTRONE

 SERVES 6   WORK TIME 1½-2 HOURS   BAKING TIME ¾-1 HOUR

EQUIPMENT

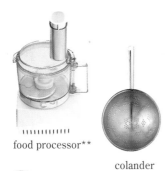
food processor**

slotted spoon

colander

bowls

cheese grater

saucepans

wooden spoon

small knife

ladle

vegetable peeler   chef's knife

rubber spatula

chopping board

**blender can also be used

INGREDIENTS

zucchini

dried red
kidney beans

green beans

dried white
kidney beans

garlic cloves

fresh basil

green peas

elbow
macaroni

potatoes

Parmesan
cheese

tomatoes

olive oil   carrots

A purée of tomato, garlic, and basil is stirred in at the finish to give a burst of fresh flavor to Genoese-style minestrone.

GETTING AHEAD
The soup and sauce can be made 1 day ahead and refrigerated separately; reheat soup before adding sauce.
* plus 8 hours soaking time

SHOPPING LIST

1 cup	dried red kidney beans
1 cup	dried white kidney beans
4 oz	elbow macaroni
6 oz	green beans
3	medium carrots, total weight about 8 oz
3	medium potatoes, total weight about 12 oz
1	medium zucchini
1 cup	shelled green peas or defrosted peas
	salt and pepper
2 quarts	water
1 cup	grated Parmesan cheese for sprinkling
	For the tomato pesto sauce
2	medium tomatoes
1	large bunch of fresh basil
4	garlic cloves
1 tsp	salt
	pepper
¾ cup	olive oil

ORDER OF WORK

1 PREPARE THE DRIED BEANS AND MACARONI

2 MAKE THE VEGETABLE SOUP

3 MAKE THE TOMATO PESTO SAUCE

4 FINISH THE SOUP

1 PREPARE THE DRIED BEANS AND MACARONI

Water washes away starch so pasta does not stick together

1 Put the red and white dried beans in separate bowls. Add water to cover generously and leave them to soak overnight. Drain the beans, rinse with cold water, and drain again.

ANNE SAYS
"Rather than soaking the beans overnight, you can put them in 2 medium saucepans with water to cover, bring to a boil, and let simmer 1 hour, adding more water if necessary so the beans are always covered."

2 Put the beans in separate saucepans, add water to cover generously, and bring to a boil. Reduce the heat and simmer. Season with salt and pepper halfway through cooking. Cook the beans until tender but still slightly firm when gently squeezed, about 1½ hours. Drain thoroughly.

! TAKE CARE !
Salt added at the beginning of cooking toughens the skin of dried beans.

3 Fill a medium saucepan with water, bring to a boil, and add salt. Add the macaroni and cook until just tender, stirring occasionally, 5-7 minutes. Drain and rinse with hot water, then set aside.

2 MAKE THE VEGETABLE SOUP

1 Break the ends off the green beans and cut the beans into ½-inch pieces. Peel the carrots and potatoes; trim the ends from the zucchini. Cut the carrots, potatoes, and zucchini into dice (see box, right).

Chef's knife helps you dice quickly

HOW TO DICE VEGETABLES

1 Peel or trim the vegetable, then square off the sides if necessary. Cut vertically into ½-inch slices.

2 Stack the slices together and cut downward through the slices to make ½-inch strips.

3 Gather the strips together into a pile and cut them crosswise to produce even ½-inch dice.

Keep fingers out of blade's way

Add green peas to colorful mixture of vegetables in pan

2 Put the cooked kidney beans in a large saucepan and add the green beans, carrots, potatoes, zucchini, peas, and a little salt and pepper.

3 Add the water and bring to a boil, then reduce the heat and simmer over low heat until the vegetables are very tender, 1 hour. Meanwhile, make the tomato pesto sauce.

3 MAKE THE TOMATO PESTO SAUCE

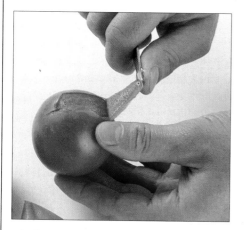

Strike garlic clove to loosen skin

Set aside basil sprigs for herb garnish

1 Score an "x" on the base of each tomato. Immerse them in boiling water until skin starts to split. Transfer to cold water, then peel. Halve the tomatoes, squeeze out seeds, and chop.

2 Strip the leaves from the basil stems, reserving 6 sprigs. Set the flat side of the chef's knife on top of each garlic clove and strike it with your fist. Discard skin.

3 Put the garlic, basil leaves, and chopped tomatoes, salt, and a little pepper in the food processor and purée until the mixture is smooth.

Tomatoes add flavor and help stabilize the sauce

4 With the blades turning, gradually add the oil. Scrape down the sides of the processor bowl from time to time with the rubber spatula. Taste the sauce for seasoning.

4 FINISH THE SOUP

Pesto sauce flavors soup and thickens it slightly

1 Add the macaroni to the vegetable soup and taste for seasoning. Gently reheat the soup to boiling. Remove the saucepan from the heat, and stir the tomato pesto sauce into the minestrone soup.

Freshly grated Parmesan cheese enhances flavor of vegetables

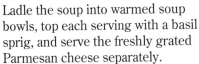

🍴 TO SERVE

Ladle the soup into warmed soup bowls, top each serving with a basil sprig, and serve the freshly grated Parmesan cheese separately.

Vegetables in minestrone are meltingly tender

V A R I A T I O N

SOUPE AU PISTOU, CROUTES GRATINEES

With a few changes, Genoese Minestrone becomes the famous French soup, Pistou.

1 Cook the dried beans and macaroni, and make the vegetable soup as directed, omitting the peas.

2 Make the tomato pesto sauce as directed.

3 Heat the oven to 350° F. Make toasted cheese croûtes: Cut 1 small loaf of French bread (weighing about 6 oz) into 3/4-inch slices; you should have 24 slices. Spread the slices of French bread on a baking sheet.

4 Brush the slices lightly with 2-3 tbsp olive oil and sprinkle with 1/2 cup grated Parmesan cheese. Bake until crisp, about 5 minutes.

5 Stir the pesto sauce into the hot soup, ladle into warmed bowls, and float a croûte on each serving. Pass remaining croûtes separately. Omit the grated Parmesan cheese for sprinkling.

BORSCHT WITH PIROSHKI

🍽 SERVES 8-10 🥣 WORK TIME 50-55 MINUTES* 🍲 BAKING TIME 1-1¼ HOURS

EQUIPMENT

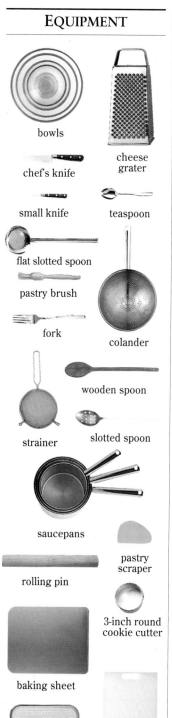

- bowls
- cheese grater
- chef's knife
- small knife
- teaspoon
- flat slotted spoon
- pastry brush
- fork
- colander
- wooden spoon
- strainer
- slotted spoon
- saucepans
- pastry scraper
- rolling pin
- 3-inch round cookie cutter
- baking sheet
- plate
- chopping board

Borscht is the classic soup of Eastern Europe and 'piroshki,' little savory turnovers, are the traditional accompaniment.

* plus 45 minutes chilling time

SHOPPING LIST

1	medium head of white cabbage, weighing about 3 lb
2	medium carrots, total weight about 5 oz
3	medium onions, total weight about 8 oz
	a few sprigs of fresh dill
	a few sprigs of parsley
1½ lb	tomatoes
6	medium beets, total weight about 2 lb
	salt and pepper
¼ cup	butter
2 quarts	chicken stock (see box, page 47) or water, more if needed
1 tsp	sugar, more to taste
	juice of 1 lemon
2-3 tbsp	red wine vinegar
¼ cup	farmer's or pot cheese
2 tsp	caraway seeds
½ cup	sour cream
	For the sour cream dough
1½ cups	flour
1	egg
¼ cup	unsalted butter
2 tbsp	sour cream
1	egg for glaze

INGREDIENTS

- white cabbage
- carrots
- tomatoes
- fresh dill
- beets
- chicken stock
- parsley
- sugar
- flour
- red wine vinegar
- butter
- lemon juice
- sour cream
- caraway seeds
- farmer's cheese
- eggs
- onions

ORDER OF WORK

1 PREPARE THE VEGETABLES

2 MAKE THE SOUR CREAM DOUGH

3 MAKE THE BORSCHT

4 FILL AND BAKE THE PIROSHKI

1 PREPARE THE VEGETABLES

1 Trim the cabbage, discard any wilted leaves, and cut in half. Cut a wedge around the core in each half and remove. Set the cabbage halves cut-side down and finely shred. Discard any thick ribs. Set aside ½ cup of the shredded cabbage for the piroshki.

Reserve cabbage for stuffing piroshki

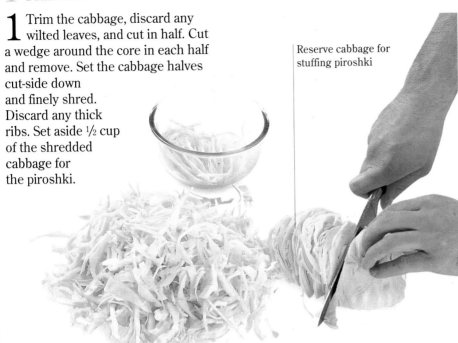

2 Peel the carrots and trim off the ends. Cut each carrot into 4 pieces. Cut each piece lengthwise into ¼-inch slices. Stack the slices and cut each stack into 4-6 strips. Gather the strips together into a pile and cut across them to form medium chopped carrots.

3 Peel the onions, leaving a little of the root attached, and cut them in half. Slice each half horizontally toward the root, leaving the slices attached at the root end, and then slice vertically, again leaving the root end uncut. Finally, cut across to make dice.

4 Strip the dill and parsley leaves from the stems and pile them on the chopping board. With the chef's knife, finely chop the leaves.

5 Cut the cores from the tomatoes and score an "x" on the base of each with the tip of a knife. Immerse them in a saucepan of boiling water until the skin starts to split, 8-15 seconds depending on their ripeness. Using the slotted spoon, transfer them at once to a bowl of cold water. When cold, peel off the skin. Cut the tomatoes crosswise in half and squeeze out the seeds, then coarsely chop each half.

Let tomatoes cool before handling

Hot water makes tomato skins split

6 Trim and scrub the beets. Half-fill a pan with water, add salt, then the beets, and bring to a boil. Cook until tender when tested with tip of the small knife, about 30 minutes. Meanwhile, make the sour cream dough.

! TAKE CARE !
Never peel beets before cooking because they "bleed."

7 Drain the beets. When cool enough to handle, peel off the skin. Grate onto the plate.

2 MAKE THE SOUR CREAM DOUGH

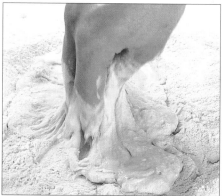

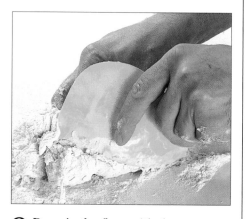

1 Sift the flour onto a work surface and make a well in the center. Put the egg and 1/2 tsp salt in the well. Using the rolling pin, pound the butter to soften it slightly and add it to the well, then add the sour cream.

2 With your fingertips, work together the egg, salt, butter, and sour cream in the well until the ingredients are thoroughly mixed.

3 Draw in the flour with the pastry scraper. With your fingers, work the flour into the other ingredients until coarse crumbs form. Press the dough into a ball.

ANNE SAYS
"If the dough is very dry, sprinkle it with 1-2 tbsp water."

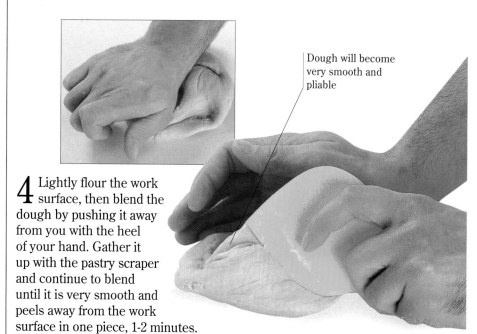

Dough will become very smooth and pliable

4 Lightly flour the work surface, then blend the dough by pushing it away from you with the heel of your hand. Gather it up with the pastry scraper and continue to blend until it is very smooth and peels away from the work surface in one piece, 1-2 minutes.

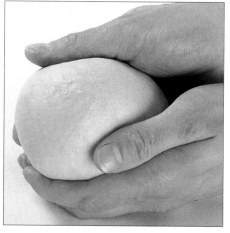

5 Shape the sour cream dough into a ball, wrap it tightly, and chill until firm, about 30 minutes.

3 MAKE THE BORSCHT

1 Melt the butter in a large saucepan. Add the chopped carrots and diced onions and cook, stirring, until soft but not brown, 3-5 minutes. Set aside one quarter of the sautéed vegetables for the piroshki filling.

2 Add the cabbage, beets, tomatoes, stock, salt, pepper, and sugar to taste, to the saucepan and bring to a boil. Simmer 45-60 minutes. Taste for seasoning and add more stock if the borscht is too thick. Set aside while you fill and bake the piroshki.

3 Just before serving, reheat the borscht if necessary. Stir in the chopped herbs, lemon juice, and red wine vinegar, and taste for seasoning.

HOW TO MAKE CHICKEN STOCK

Indispensable in many sauce and soup recipes, chicken stock keeps well up to 3 days, covered, in the refrigerator and it also freezes well. The longer stock simmers the more flavor it has, and it is often reduced to concentrate, so salt and pepper are not added during cooking.

 MAKES ABOUT 2 QUARTS

 WORK TIME 15 MINUTES

 COOKING TIME UP TO 3 HOURS

SHOPPING LIST

1	stewing chicken, or 2 lb raw chicken backs and necks
1	onion
1	carrot
1	celery stalk
1	bouquet garni made with 5-6 parsley stems, 2-3 fresh thyme sprigs, and 1 bay leaf
1/2-1 tsp	peppercorns
2 quarts	water, more if needed

1 Put the chicken in a large pot. Peel and quarter the onion and carrot; quarter the celery. Add to the pot with the bouquet garni and peppercorns.

2 Add water just to cover the ingredients. Bring to a boil and simmer up to 3 hours, skimming the stock occasionally.

3 If using a stewing chicken, remove it when the thigh is tender when pierced with a skewer, 1¼-1¾ hours. The meat can then be used in a recipe calling for cooked chicken.

Strain to remove flavoring ingredients

4 Using a ladle, strain the stock into a large bowl.

4 FILL AND BAKE THE PIROSHKI

1 Make the filling: Put the reserved shredded cabbage in a bowl. Cover it generously with boiling water and leave 2 minutes. Drain, rinse with cold water, and drain again thoroughly, squeezing out excess water if necessary. Coarsely chop it.

2 Stir the chopped cabbage, farmer's cheese, and caraway seeds into the reserved carrots and onions. Season with salt and pepper.

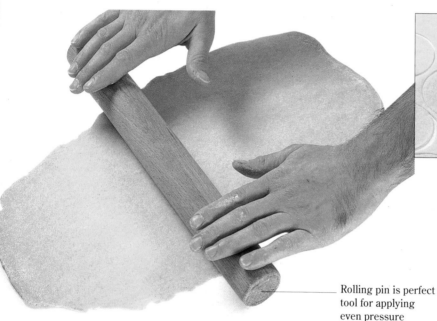

Rolling pin is perfect tool for applying even pressure

3 Lightly flour the work surface. Roll out the sour cream dough about 1/8 inch thick. Cut out rounds from the dough with the cookie cutter or a sharp-edged glass.

ANNE SAYS
"You should have 25-30 rounds. If necessary, roll out the scraps and cut out additional rounds."

Push filling from spoon with finger or another spoon

4 To make the egg glaze, lightly beat the egg with 1/2 tsp salt.

5 Using the teaspoon put a spoonful of filling in the center of each dough round. Brush the edge of each round with a little egg glaze.

! TAKE CARE !
Do not overfill piroshki or they will burst during cooking.

6 Take one dough round in your fingers, lift the dough to meet on top of the filling, and pinch the edges together to seal. Transfer the piroshki to the baking sheet and brush with the egg glaze. Chill 15 minutes. Heat the oven to 400° F.

Piroshki should be evenly browned

7 Bake the piroshki in the heated oven until golden brown, 15-18 minutes. Let them cool slightly while you finish the borscht.

Piroshki have tempting golden brown glaze when cooked

🍴 TO SERVE
Pour the soup into a warmed tureen and top with the sour cream. Pass the piroshki separately.

Sour cream is stirred into borscht before serving to add richness

Piroshki are stuffed with cheese and vegetable mixture

VARIATION
RUSTIC BORSCHT

This hearty variation of Borscht with Piroshki includes beef and its stock.

1 Put a piece of beef shank with bone (weighing about 3 lb) in a kettle and add plenty of water to cover and a little salt. Bring to a boil, then simmer the beef, skimming occasionally, until very tender, 3-4 hours.
2 Prepare the borscht as directed in the main recipe, using a small head of cabbage (weighing about 2 lb) and 2 onions, omitting the tomatoes, and using the beef and its liquid instead of chicken stock.
3 Meanwhile, peel, seed, and finely chop 1 tomato. Make the piroshki as directed, adding the chopped tomato to the stuffing.
4 Remove the beef from the borscht. Shred the beef using 2 forks and return it to the soup, discarding the bone. Flavor the borscht with lemon juice and red wine vinegar and serve in individual bowls, topped with the sour cream and chopped herbs.

GETTING AHEAD
The borscht can be prepared and kept, covered, in the refrigerator 2-3 days; the flavor improves on standing. It can also be frozen. The piroshki can be baked up to 24 hours ahead and kept in an airtight container, or can be frozen. Reheat in a 350° F oven 10 minutes.

PUMPKIN STEW

🍴 SERVES 6 🥄 WORK TIME 50-60 MINUTES 🍲 BAKING TIME 2½-3 HOURS

EQUIPMENT

chef's knife

vegetable peeler

small knife

food processor*

large metal spoon

citrus juicer

wooden spoon

rubber spatula

large baking dish**

colander

bowls

saucepan

slotted spoon

ladle

heatproof casserole***

*blender can also be used
**roasting pan can also be used
***large pot can also be used

Stews suggest hearty meals and this one is no exception. A bright orange pumpkin is hollowed out, and its flesh cooked with leeks, tomatoes, and turnips. The stew is then returned to the pumpkin shell for an attractive presentation.

SHOPPING LIST

1	pumpkin, weighing about 12 lb
2 quarts	boiling water
3	medium leeks
2	celery stalks
2	garlic cloves
4	medium tomatoes, total weight about 1 lb
6 oz	bacon
3-5	sprigs of fresh thyme
1	butternut squash, weighing about 1½ lb
1	celery root, weighing about 1½ lb
	juice of ½ lemon
5	medium turnips, total weight about 1 lb
1	medium zucchini
½ cup	butter
¼ cup	flour
2 cups	chicken stock, more if needed
	salt and pepper
	cayenne
	sage biscuits (see box, page 54) for serving (optional)

INGREDIENTS

pumpkin

celery root

butter

zucchini

leeks

lemon juice

butternut squash

bacon

celery stalks

flour

chicken stock

turnips

fresh thyme

tomatoes   garlic cloves   cayenne

ORDER OF WORK

1 PREPARE THE PUMPKIN SHELL

2 PREPARE THE INGREDIENTS FOR THE STEW

3 MAKE THE STEW

1 PREPARE THE PUMPKIN SHELL

1 Heat the oven to 325° F. Cut around the stem-end of the pumpkin at an angle and pull off the round "lid." Set the lid aside.

2 Scoop out the seeds with all the fibrous threads and discard them.

ANNE SAYS
"Your hands are the best tools for this."

3 Put the pumpkin in the baking dish. Pour enough boiling water into the pumpkin to fill it. Replace the stem end and bake until the flesh is just tender, 1½-2 hours.

4 Ladle out and discard the cooking water. With the large spoon, scoop out the flesh without piercing the shell of the pumpkin; the shell should be about ½-inch thick. Set the shell aside and cut the flesh into chunks.

Use ladle to remove water from hot pumpkin

5 Purée the pumpkin chunks in the food processor until smooth.

ANNE SAYS
"You may have to do this in several batches."

2 PREPARE THE INGREDIENTS FOR THE STEW

1 Trim the leeks, discarding the roots and the tough green tops. Slit the leeks lengthwise, put them in the colander, and wash them thoroughly under running water.

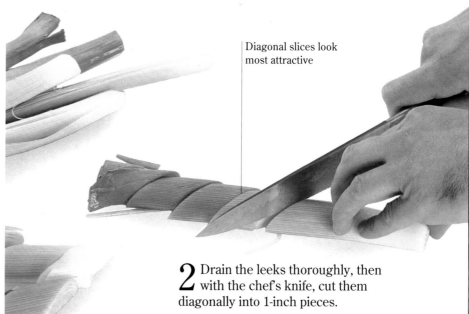

Diagonal slices look most attractive

2 Drain the leeks thoroughly, then with the chef's knife, cut them diagonally into 1-inch pieces.

3 Peel the strings from the celery with the vegetable peeler, then cut the stalks into 1/2-inch slices.

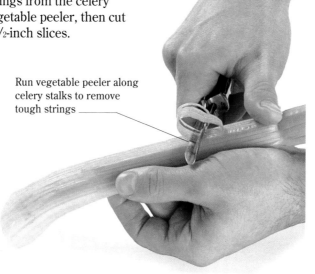

Run vegetable peeler along celery stalks to remove tough strings

4 Set the flat side of the chef's knife on top of each garlic clove and strike it with your fist. Discard the skin and finely chop the garlic.

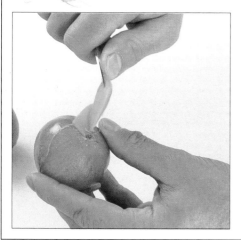

5 Cut the cores from the tomatoes and score an "x" on the base of each with the tip of the small knife. Immerse them in a pan of boiling water until the skin starts to split. Transfer them at once to a bowl of cold water. When cold, peel off the skin. Cut crosswise in half and squeeze out the seeds, then cut each half into quarters.

6 Cut the bacon crosswise into wide strips. For quick cutting, stack the bacon slices.

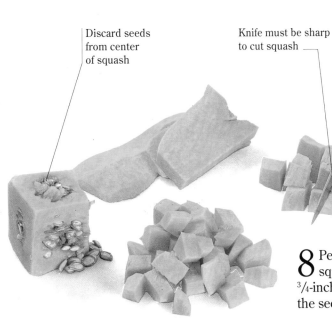

Discard seeds from center of squash

Knife must be sharp to cut squash

7 Strip the thyme leaves from the stems and pile them on the chopping board. With the chef's knife, finely chop the leaves.

8 Peel the butternut squash and cut it into $^3/_4$-inch cubes, discarding the seeds.

9 Peel the celery root with the small knife. Square off the sides and cut vertically into 1-inch slices.

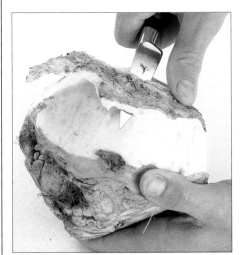

10 Stack the slices and cut them into 1-inch strips. Gather the strips together and cut across into 1-inch cubes. Put the cubes of celery root in a large bowl of water acidulated with the lemon juice, so the cubes do not become brown.

11 Peel the turnips with the vegetable peeler and cut into cubes as for the celery root.

Set slices flat-side down when cutting cubes

Remove all green when peeling

12 Trim the zucchini and cut into cubes as for the celery root.

SAGE BISCUITS

🍴 MAKES ABOUT 6

🥣 WORK TIME 30 MINUTES

🍲 COOKING TIME 12-15 MINUTES

SHOPPING LIST

	butter and flour for baking sheet
8-12	large fresh sage leaves
2 cups	flour
1 tsp	baking soda
1 tbsp	baking powder
1/2 tsp	salt
1/4 cup	vegetable shortening or unsalted butter
3/4 cup	milk, more if needed
1 tsp	cream of tartar

1 Heat the oven to 425° F. Butter and flour a baking sheet. Put the fresh sage leaves in piles of about 4 leaves on a chopping board and chop them with a chef's knife.

2 Sift the flour into a bowl with the baking soda, baking powder, and salt and make a well in the center. Add the shortening and cut it into small pieces using 2 round-bladed knives.

3 Rub the mixture with your fingertips until it forms fine crumbs, lifting and crumbling to aerate it. Make a well in the center and add the chopped sage.

Mix lightly with knife so crumbs form

4 Mix the milk and cream of tartar together and add to the well. Toss quickly to form crumbs. Do not overmix or the biscuits will be heavy.

5 Turn the biscuit dough onto a floured surface and knead lightly for a few seconds – the dough should remain quite rough.

6 Pat the dough out to 3/4-inch thickness. Cut out rounds with a 2 1/2 -inch round cookie cutter, then pat out the trimmings and cut additional rounds, for a total of six. Transfer each dough round to the prepared baking sheet as it is cut.

7 Bake in the heated oven until lightly browned, 12-15 minutes. Transfer them to a wire rack to cool.

3 MAKE THE STEW

1 Heat the butter in the large pot, add the bacon, and cook, stirring, until lightly browned, 3-5 minutes. Add the leeks and garlic and soften over low heat, stirring occasionally, 3-5 minutes. Add the flour and cook, stirring, until foaming, 1-2 minutes.

2 Stir in the stock and pumpkin purée. Drain the celery root and add it to the pot with salt, pepper, and cayenne to taste. Bring to a boil and simmer 20 minutes. Add the celery slices and cubed turnips and simmer 20 minutes longer.

3 Add the squash and zucchini cubes, the tomatoes, and thyme and simmer 10 minutes. Taste for seasoning.

Tender vegetables are added last

🍴 TO SERVE

Ladle the stew into the pumpkin shell set on a serving plate. Warm sage biscuits can be served on the side.

Pumpkin shell is impressive serving container for stew

Sage biscuits make pumpkin stew a substantial meal

VARIATION

PUMPKIN STEW WITH ONION TOPPING

Here the pumpkin stew is served in individual dishes with a topping of fried onions and bacon.

1 Prepare the pumpkin purée as directed; discard the pumpkin shell.
2 Prepare the vegetables and bacon as directed, increasing the quantity of bacon to 9 oz.
3 After browning the bacon, remove and reserve one-third for the topping. Continue making the stew as directed.
4 Peel 3 medium onions and cut them vertically into thin slices to produce rings. Toss to coat them in $1/4$ cup flour seasoned with salt and pepper. Heat $1/4$ cup oil in a large frying pan, add the onions, and cook, stirring, until browned, 2-3 minutes. Cook the onions in batches if necessary to ensure that they will brown nicely. Transfer them to paper towels to drain.
5 Ladle the stew into individual bowls, sprinkle with the reserved bacon and browned onions, and decorate the stew with flat-leaved parsley sprigs.

GETTING AHEAD

The pumpkin stew can be made up to 2 days in advance and refrigerated. Reheat it on top of the stove and transfer it to the pumpkin shell just before serving.

MEDITERRANEAN VEGETABLE PLATTER WITH GARLIC SAUCE

Grand Aïoli

 SERVES 8   WORK TIME 50-60 MINUTES   BAKING TIME 65-70 MINUTES

EQUIPMENT

 saucepans

 vegetable peeler

 heatproof plate

whisk

kitchen scissors

 food processor*

teaspoon

 colander

vegetable brush

small knife

chef's knife

bowls

2-pronged fork

 kitchen string

paper towels

 serrated knife

*blender can also be used

For "le grand aïoli," a plethora of cold cooked Provençal vegetables are served on a platter, accompanied by a zesty garlic-herb sauce. In Marseille, this dish is traditionally served on Ash Wednesday, and ingredients such as squid, salt cod, or snails may be added.

GETTING AHEAD

The eggs can be boiled and the sauce made up to 2 days ahead and refrigerated. If you like, cook the vegetables up to 6 hours ahead and keep at room temperature.

SHOPPING LIST

8	eggs
8	baby or medium globe artichokes
1	lemon
1 lb	baby carrots or medium carrots
4	fennel bulbs
1 lb	new potatoes
1 lb	asparagus
For the garlic-herb sauce	
2	eggs
5-7	sprigs of fresh herbs such as tarragon and parsley
1½ tbsp	butter
1½ tbsp	flour
½ cup	boiling water
4	garlic cloves, or to taste
¼ cup	olive oil
	salt and pepper

INGREDIENTS

 globe artichokes

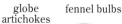 fennel bulbs

 olive oil

 new potatoes

lemon

fresh herbs

carrots

 asparagus

 garlic cloves

eggs

 butter

flour

ORDER OF WORK

1 MAKE THE GARLIC-HERB SAUCE

2 PREPARE AND COOK THE ARTICHOKES

3 PREPARE AND COOK THE CARROTS, FENNEL, AND POTATOES

4 PREPARE AND COOK THE ASPARAGUS

1 MAKE THE GARLIC-HERB SAUCE

Put eggs in cold water after cooking to help loosen shell

1 Put all 10 eggs in a pan of cold water, bring to a boil, and simmer 10 minutes. Drain the eggs.

2 Transfer to a bowl of cold water, and let cool. Tap the eggs to crack, then peel. Rinse with cold water. Set 8 eggs aside in cold water.

3 Cut the remaining 2 eggs in half and separate the yolks. Discard the whites or set them aside for another use. Strip herb leaves from stems, reserving a few sprigs for decoration.

4 Melt the butter in a small saucepan. Whisk in the flour and cook until foaming, about 1 minute.

5 Remove from the heat and whisk in the boiling water. Return to a medium heat and cook, stirring, until the sauce reaches a boil and thickens.

! TAKE CARE !
Whisk constantly to ensure the mixture is smooth.

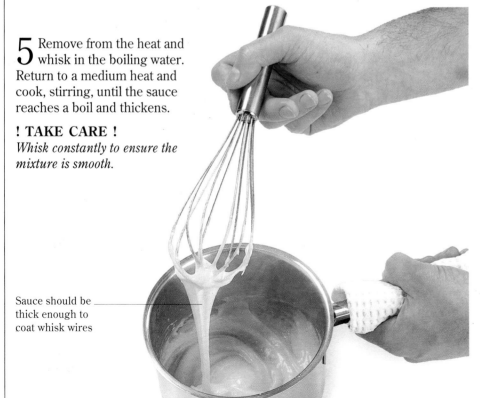

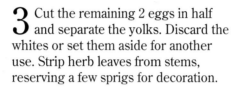

Sauce should be thick enough to coat whisk wires

6 Transfer the sauce to the food processor and add the hard-boiled egg yolks, peeled garlic cloves, and herb leaves. Purée until smooth. With the blades turning, gradually pour in the olive oil, so the sauce becomes creamy. Taste for seasoning, then transfer to a serving bowl.

2 PREPARE AND COOK THE ARTICHOKES

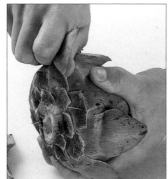

1 If using medium globe artichokes, prepare the bottoms (see box, below). If using baby artichokes, trim the stems, leaving about 2 inches. Pull off 2-3 rows of the tough, green, lower leaves, cutting them if necessary. The remaining leaves should be tender.

Rub artichokes with lemon juice to prevent discoloration

2 With the serrated knife, cut off the cone-shaped top of each baby artichoke, but leave the stem attached to the base. Cut the lemon in half and rub the cut or torn surfaces of each artichoke as it is prepared.

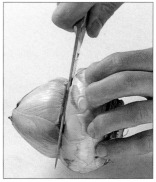

3 With the small knife, peel the stem of each baby artichoke and trim the base of the stem so it is smooth.

HOW TO PREPARE GLOBE ARTICHOKE BOTTOMS

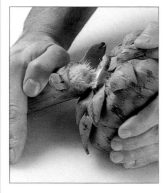

1 Snap the stem from a globe artichoke so that the fibers are pulled out with the stem.

2 Snap off the largest bottom leaves of the artichoke with your hands.

3 Using a very sharp knife, cut off all large bottom leaves, leaving a cone of soft small leaves in the center.

4 Cut off the soft cone of leaves; discard, leaving only the choke behind.

5 Trim the bottom of any remaining dark green parts, then trim to an even shape, slightly flattened at the base with the top edge bevelled. Rub well with a cut lemon to prevent discoloration. Immerse the artichoke bottom in a bowl of water, acidulated with the juice of 1/2 lemon, and set aside until ready to cook.

3 PREPARE AND COOK THE CARROTS, FENNEL, AND POTATOES

4 With the serrated knife, cut very small baby artichokes in half and larger baby ones into quarters. Rub all the cut or torn surfaces of the artichoke pieces with the cut lemon again.

1 If the baby carrots have green tops, trim them, leaving about ¼ inch of green. Scrape the carrots with the small knife to remove the thin skin. If using medium carrots, peel them, then quarter them lengthwise.

ANNE SAYS
"Use a vegetable peeler only if carrots are mature, with a thick skin."

2 Rinse the carrots, put them in a saucepan of cold water, add salt, and bring to a boil. Simmer until just tender, 8-10 minutes. Test with the tip of the small knife. Drain the carrots in the colander, rinse with cold water, and drain again thoroughly.

5 Bring a saucepan of water to a boil. Add salt, then the baby artichokes or artichoke bottoms and weigh them down with the heatproof plate so they are submerged. Simmer until tender, 20-25 minutes for baby artichokes or 15-20 minutes for artichoke bottoms.

3 Trim the tops and bases of the fennel bulbs to remove stems and any dry ends. Discard any tough outer pieces.

Cut off any stem from fennel bulb

Trim any dry ends from tops of bulbs

6 Drain the artichokes in the colander and let cool to tepid. With the teaspoon, scoop out the chokes, removing also tough inner purple leaves from baby artichokes. Cut artichoke bottoms into quarters.

4 Cut each fennel bulb lengthwise into quarters. Bring a saucepan of water to a boil, add salt, then the fennel, and simmer until just tender, 12-15 minutes. Drain the fennel in the colander, rinse with cold water, and drain again thoroughly.

5 Rinse the potatoes, scrubbing them gently to remove any dirt. Cut larger potatoes in half.

ANNE SAYS
"So the potatoes cook in the same time, they should be of uniform size."

6 Put the potatoes in a saucepan of cold water, add salt, and bring to a boil. Simmer until they are just tender, 12-15 minutes. Drain the potatoes in the colander, rinse with cold water, and drain again thoroughly.

4 PREPARE AND COOK THE ASPARAGUS

1 Using the vegetable peeler, strip away the tough, outer skin at the bottom of each asparagus stem. Trim off woody ends, if necessary. If the asparagus is young and the spears slender, they do not need peeling.

Work from tip of asparagus spear toward base

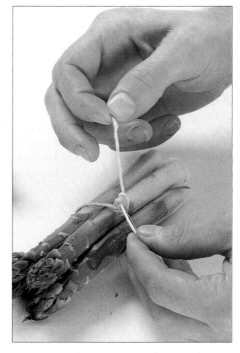

2 With the kitchen string, tie the asparagus into bundles of 5-7 spears each. Bring a shallow pan of water to a boil, add salt, then the asparagus bundles and simmer until just tender, 5-6 minutes.

ANNE SAYS
"Use a shallow, wide pan so that the asparagus can lie flat."

3 Using the 2-pronged fork, transfer the asparagus bundles to the colander, rinse with cold water, and drain on paper towels.

Lift asparagus into colander carefully so spears do not break

VARIATION

VEGETABLE SALAD WITH TAHINI DRESSING

In this variation of Grand Aïoli, the same vegetables are served with a Middle-Eastern sauce. Tahini is available in specialty or Middle-Eastern food shops.

🍽 TO SERVE

Drain and dry the remaining hard-boiled eggs and cut them in half. Arrange the vegetables in sections on a large serving platter. Add the eggs. Decorate with the reserved herb sprigs and serve at room temperature with the bowl of garlic-herb sauce.

Garlic-herb sauce can be as garlicky as you like, according to how many garlic cloves are used

1 Prepare and cook the vegetables, and hard-boil and prepare 8 eggs, as directed in the main recipe.

2 To make the tahini dressing: Purée 2 garlic cloves in a food processor or blender. Add ½ cup tahini paste with the juice of 1 lemon (about ¼ cup) and a generous pinch of salt. Purée until the mixture is smooth, then add water a teaspoon at a time until the sauce reaches the consistency of sour cream.

3 Arrange the vegetables on individual plates with 2 egg halves each and the tahini sauce in small bowls in the center. Accompany with toasted wedges of pita bread, if you like.

Globe artichokes and bulb fennel are typical Provençal vegetables

STUFFED VEGETABLE TRIO WITH WALNUT-GARLIC SAUCE

 SERVES 4 　 WORK TIME 40-45 MINUTES* 　 BAKING TIME 15-20 MINUTES

EQUIPMENT

bowls

chef's knife

food processor

melon baller**

small knife

wooden spoon

slotted spoon

rubber spatula

large baking dish

teaspoon

vegetable peeler

frying pan

aluminum foil

large saucepan with lid

pastry brush

paper towels

metal spoon

colander

**teaspoon can also be used

INGREDIENTS

zucchini

parsley

fresh shiitake mushrooms

fresh tarragon

bulghur

garlic cloves

large tomatoes

large red onions

celery stalks

vegetable oil

walnut halves

walnut oil

Sweet onions, zucchini, and plump ripe tomatoes are hollowed and filled with a grain-based stuffing, then served with a walnut-garlic sauce. Coarse-grained bulghur (cracked wheat) is best for the stuffing, but kasha can be substituted.

* plus 30 minutes standing time

SHOPPING LIST

4	large tomatoes, total weight about 1¹/₂ lb
	salt and pepper
4	large red onions, total weight about 1¹/₂ lb
2	medium zucchini, total weight about 1 lb
1¹/₂ cups	bulghur
3 cups	boiling water
2	celery stalks
4 oz	fresh shiitake or common mushrooms
4	garlic cloves
4-6	sprigs of fresh tarragon
4-6	sprigs of parsley
3 tbsp	vegetable oil, more for baking dish and foil
	For the walnut-garlic sauce
4-6	sprigs of parsley
²/₃ cup	walnut halves
4	garlic cloves
2 tbsp	cold water
1 cup	walnut oil

ORDER OF WORK

1 PREPARE THE VEGETABLES

2 MAKE THE BULGHUR STUFFING

3 STUFF AND BAKE THE VEGETABLES

4 MAKE THE WALNUT-GARLIC SAUCE

1 PREPARE THE VEGETABLES

1 With the small knife, core the tomatoes. If necessary, cut a thin slice from the base of each one so it will sit flat.

2 Cut a slice from the top of each tomato. Scoop out the tomato seeds and flesh with the teaspoon, leaving a ³/₈-inch wall of flesh. Scrape the seeds from the scooped-out flesh; reserve the tomato flesh for the stuffing. Season the inside of the tomatoes with salt and pepper, then set them upside down on paper towels and let drain 30 minutes.

3 Peel the onions with the small knife. Cut a flat slice from the top and a thin slice from the root end of each onion so it will sit flat.

Deep purple-red onions have mild flavor

Discard papery skins

4 Put the onions in the saucepan and add water to cover. Add salt, put on the lid, and bring to a boil. Simmer until barely tender, 10-15 minutes. Drain the onions on paper towels.

5 When cool enough to handle, hollow out the onions, leaving a ³/₈-inch wall of onion, by pushing out the core with your fingers. Reserve the onion cores for the stuffing.

6 Trim the zucchini and cut them lengthwise in half. Blanch the zucchini: Fill the saucepan with fresh water, bring to a boil, add salt, and then the zucchini. Simmer 3-5 minutes. Drain in the colander and rinse with cold water.

Use melon baller or teaspoon to remove seeds neatly

7 Scoop out and discard the seeds from each of the courgette halves leaving a 3/8-inch shell of zucchini flesh round the edge.

2 MAKE THE BULGHUR STUFFING

1 Put the bulghur in a large bowl, pour on the boiling water, cover, and let stand until plump, 30 minutes. Drain off any excess water.

2 Peel the strings from the celery stalks with the vegetable peeler and cut across into thin slices.

With mushrooms stem-side down, cut caps into rough quarters

3 Wipe the shiitake mushrooms with a damp paper towel and trim the stems. Cut the mushrooms into quarters, then chop them.

ANNE SAYS
"You can chop the mushrooms in the food processor, using the pulse button, but do not overwork them or they will form a purée."

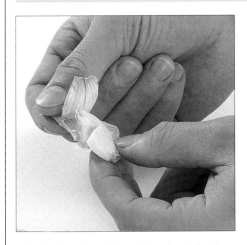

4 Set the flat side of the chef's knife on top of the garlic cloves and strike it with your fist. Discard the skin and finely chop the cloves.

5 Chop the reserved onion cores and the tomato flesh. Chop the herbs (see box, right).

HOW TO CHOP HERBS

Parsley, dill, chives, rosemary, tarragon, thyme, and basil are herbs that are usually chopped before being added to other ingredients in a recipe. They can be chopped coarsely or finely, but delicate herbs, such as tarragon and basil, bruise easily, so take care not to chop them too finely.

1 Strip the leaves or sprigs from the stems of the herbs, then pile the leaves or sprigs on a chopping board.

Fry lightly to retain crunchy texture

Add chopped vegetables to hot oil in pan

6 Heat the oil in the frying pan. Add the celery, garlic, and chopped onion and cook, stirring, until soft but not brown, 2-3 minutes.

7 Add the mushrooms with salt and pepper and continue cooking until all the liquid has evaporated, about 5 minutes longer. Stir in the chopped tomato and cook until the liquid evaporates, about 2 minutes.

2 Cut the leaves or sprigs into small pieces. Holding the tip of the blade of a chef's knife against the board and rocking the blade back and forth, continue chopping until the herbs are coarse or fine, as you wish.

ANNE SAYS
"*Make sure that your knife is very sharp, otherwise you will bruise the herbs rather than cut them.*"

8 Add the chopped herbs to the vegetables and taste for seasoning.

9 Mix the sautéed vegetables into the bulghur. Taste for seasoning.

4 MAKE THE WALNUT-GARLIC SAUCE

1 Strip the parsley sprigs from the stems and peel the garlic cloves. Purée the walnut halves, peeled garlic, parsley sprigs, and cold water in the food processor or a blender to form a paste. Season with salt and pepper.

3 STUFF AND BAKE THE VEGETABLES

1 Heat the oven to 375°F. Oil the baking dish. Spoon the bulghur stuffing into the hollows in the onions, zucchini, and tomatoes. Spread the remaining stuffing over the bottom of the oiled baking dish.

Mound stuffing well in vegetables

Pour in oil slowly

2 Arrange the vegetables on the stuffing in the dish. Cover with a piece of oiled foil, transfer to the heated oven, and bake until tender, 15-20 minutes. Meanwhile, make the walnut-garlic sauce.

2 With the blade turning, gradually add the walnut oil to the mixture.

3 Scrape down the sides of the processor bowl from time to time with the rubber spatula. When all the walnut oil has been added, taste the sauce for seasoning.

🍽 TO SERVE

Arrange a tomato, an onion, and a zucchini half, with extra stuffing from the baking dish, on each of 4 warmed individual plates. Serve the walnut-garlic sauce on the side.

Parsley sprigs are fresh decoration

WILD-RICE-STUFFED VEGETABLE TRIO

Wild rice replaces bulghur as the basis for the filling in this version of stuffed vegetables.

1 Prepare the vegetables as directed.
2 Bring 5 cups water to a boil, add salt, then stir in 2 cups wild rice. Simmer, covered, until tender, about 40 minutes. Drain. Use in place of the bulghur to make the stuffing.
3 Stuff and bake the vegetables as directed. Serve with walnut-garlic sauce, and decorate with celery leaves.

VEGETABLE TRIO WITH CARROT-RICE STUFFING

Grated carrot is a colorful addition to this trio of stuffed vegetables.

1 Prepare the vegetables as directed.
2 Cook 1¼ cups long-grain white rice in boiling salted water until barely tender, 10-12 minutes. Drain the rice in a colander and rinse with cold running water.
3 Peel and grate 2 medium carrots.
4 Make the stuffing as directed, using the rice in place of the bulghur and stirring in the grated carrot.
5 Stuff and bake the vegetables as directed and serve with the walnut-garlic sauce.

GETTING AHEAD

The vegetables can be prepared 24 hours ahead and kept, covered, in the refrigerator. Reheat them 15 minutes in an oven heated to 350° F, or serve them at room temperature.

Sauce is pungent, and perfect with stuffed vegetables

MOSAIC OF VEGETABLES WITH CHICKEN MOUSSE

🍽 SERVES 6-8 🥣 WORK TIME ABOUT 1 HOUR 🍲 BAKING TIME 1½-1¾ HOURS

EQUIPMENT

vegetable peeler

bowls

pastry brush

metal spoon

food processor*

chef's knife

11½- x 3½- x 3-inch terrine mold

frying pan

whisk

saucepans

metal spatula

colander

wooden spoon

dish towel

roasting pan

aluminum foil

rubber spatula

metal skewer

*blender can also be used

This nouvelle cuisine mosaic of vegetables, held together with a light chicken mousse, has become a classic. If you're short of time, omit the green beans and double the amount of spinach.

GETTING AHEAD

The mosaic and mustard sauce can be made up to 2 days ahead and refrigerated.

SHOPPING LIST

1 lb	spinach
	salt and white pepper
1 tbsp	softened butter, more for terrine mold
	ground nutmeg
12 oz	carrots
8 oz	green beans
	For the chicken mousse
1½ lb	boneless chicken breast halves
1	egg
3 tbsp	butter, at room temperature
¾ cup	heavy cream
	For the mustard sauce
2	eggs
1½ tbsp	butter
1½ tbsp	flour
½ cup	boiling water
1	garlic clove
3 tbsp	Dijon-style mustard
¼ cup	olive oil

INGREDIENTS

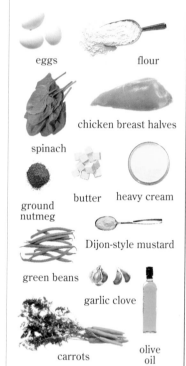

eggs

flour

chicken breast halves

spinach

ground nutmeg

butter

heavy cream

Dijon-style mustard

green beans

garlic clove

carrots

olive oil

ORDER OF WORK

1 LINE THE TERRINE MOLD

2 PREPARE THE VEGETABLES

3 MAKE THE CHICKEN MOUSSE

4 FILL AND BAKE THE TERRINE

5 MAKE THE MUSTARD SAUCE

1 LINE THE TERRINE MOLD

1 Discard the tough ribs and stems from the spinach leaves, then wash them thoroughly.

Leave no gaps between spinach leaves

2 Bring a large pan of water to a boil, add salt, then the spinach, and blanch 1 minute. Drain in the colander, rinse with cold water, and drain again thoroughly, patting it dry with the dish towel and keeping as many leaves whole as possible.

3 Thoroughly brush the terrine mold with butter. Arrange the whole spinach leaves on the bottom and sides of the mold, allowing about 2 inches of spinach to overhang the edge of the mold.

2 PREPARE THE VEGETABLES

1 Chop the remaining spinach. Heat the butter in a small pan, add the spinach, and sauté, stirring, until the moisture has evaporated, 2-3 minutes. Season with salt, pepper, and a pinch of ground nutmeg.

Cut carrot pieces into neat slices

2 Peel and trim the carrots. Cut across in half, then cut lengthwise into $^3/_8$-inch slices. Put the carrots in a saucepan of cold water, add salt, bring to a boil, and cook until tender, 7-10 minutes. Drain thoroughly.

3 Snap the ends from the green beans. Bring a pan of salted water to a boil, add the green beans, and cook until just tender, 5-7 minutes. Drain them, rinse with cold water, and drain again thoroughly. Sprinkle all the vegetables with salt and pepper.

3 MAKE THE CHICKEN MOUSSE

Add egg through feed tube

Fry mixture until browned and cooked

1 Cut the chicken breast halves into chunks, discarding any skin. Put the chunks in the food processor and purée until smooth. Add the egg and then the softened butter to the chicken, and purée to combine.

2 Transfer the mixture to a bowl and set it in a larger bowl of ice water. Beat with the wooden spoon until the mixture is chilled. Using the rubber spatula, beat in the heavy cream, a little at a time. Season with salt, white pepper, and a pinch of nutmeg.

ANNE SAYS
"It's preferable to use white pepper to ensure there will be no specks in the mousse, but black pepper can be used."

3 To test the seasoning of the chicken mixture, fry a little piece in the frying pan and then taste it. Adjust the seasoning of the remaining mixture, if necessary.

4 FILL AND BAKE THE TERRINE

Lay carrot slices neatly on mousse to make solid layer

1 Heat the oven to 350° F. Spread about one-sixth of the chicken mousse mixture evenly over the spinach leaves on the bottom of the mold, using the metal spatula.

2 Arrange one-quarter of the carrot slices lengthwise on top and cover them with a thin layer of mousse.

3 Add another layer of carrot slices and then mousse. Arrange half of the beans on top of the mousse.

4 Cover the beans with a thin layer of mousse. Spoon the spinach onto the mousse and spread it out into an even layer.

Fold spinach leaves over mousse to cover completely

5 Top with a layer of mousse, then a layer of beans. Layer the carrots with mousse in between, ending with a final layer of mousse. Fold the overhanging spinach over the top.

Push skewer into center of mosaic when testing if it is cooked

6 Cover the terrine mold with buttered foil and put it in the roasting pan. Pour in boiling water to come more than halfway up the sides of the mold to make a water bath.

7 Bake the terrine in the water bath in the heated oven until the mousse is set and the metal skewer inserted into the center is hot to the touch when withdrawn, about 1 hour. Add more water to the bath during cooking if necessary. Remove from the water bath and let stand in a warm place for 10 minutes, then let the mosaic cool completely in the mold.

5 MAKE THE MUSTARD SAUCE

Use chef's knife to chop whites finely

1 Half-fill a saucepan with cold water, add the eggs, then bring to a boil and simmer 10 minutes. Drain the eggs, then transfer to a bowl of cold water and let cool.

2 Tap the eggs to crack the shells, then peel them. Rinse the eggs with cold water. Cut them in half and put the yolks in a bowl. Finely chop the whites.

Keep processor running while adding oil

3 Melt the butter in a small saucepan. Whisk in the flour and cook until foaming, about 1 minute. Remove from the heat and whisk in the boiling water. The sauce will thicken at once. Return it to the heat and cook, stirring, for 1 minute.

ANNE SAYS
"The sauce will thicken as soon as the boiling water is added."

4 Transfer the sauce to the food processor, add the hard-boiled egg yolks, garlic, mustard, salt, and pepper, and purée until smooth.

5 With the blades turning, pour in the olive oil in a thin stream, so the sauce thickens and becomes creamy.

! TAKE CARE !
Do not add the oil too quickly, or the mixture will separate.

6 Pour the sauce into a bowl and stir in the chopped egg whites. Taste the sauce for seasoning. Cover and set the sauce aside.

ANNE SAYS
"The sauce will thicken as it sits."

Fold in egg whites with rubber spatula

🍴 **TO SERVE**
Set a serving platter, upside-down, on the terrine and invert to unmold the mosaic. Carefully cut it into slices and serve the mustard sauce separately.

Chicken mousse mixture
holds vegetables firmly together

MOSAIC OF VEGETABLES WITH CHEESE

A cheese-based mixture holds this vegetable mosaic together, and the sauce is made with red peppers.

1 Prepare and chop all of the spinach. Cut the carrots lengthwise in half, then into thin strips; cook as directed. Prepare and cook the green beans as directed. Grate 8 oz Gruyère cheese.
2 Sprinkle 1 tbsp powdered unflavored gelatin over ½ cup cold water and let stand until spongy, about 5 minutes.
3 Whisk together 1½ cups heavy cream, 5 egg yolks, salt, pepper, and a pinch of nutmeg. Heat the gelatin until melted. Stir it into the cream mixture.
4 Layer the carrots and beans in the terrine, with the spinach in a cylinder shape in the middle, and a little of the grated cheese and the cream mixture between each layer. Do not pack down.
5 Poke the mosaic with a skewer; pour over the remaining cream mixture.
6 Cover and bake in the water bath as directed, 1½-2 hours. Let cool completely, then refrigerate.
7 To make the sauce: Peel, core, and seed 1½ lb red bell peppers, then cut into chunks. Peel, seed, and chop 1 lb tomatoes. Chop 1 garlic clove, 2 scallions, and a small bunch of basil leaves. Heat 2 tbsp olive oil in a frying pan, add all the ingredients, and cook, stirring, until thickened, 15-20 minutes. Purée in a food processor until almost smooth. Season to taste.
8 Unmold the mosaic serve with the cold red pepper sauce.

CABBAGE WITH CHESTNUT AND PORK STUFFING

 SERVES 6 ⚱ WORK TIME 35-40 MINUTES ♨ COOKING TIME 50-60 MINUTES

EQUIPMENT

string

paper towels

food processor

fork

vegetable peeler

heatproof plate

wooden spoon

saucepans, 1 with lid

small ladle

colander

dish towel*

bowls

frying pan   strainer

grater

slotted spoon

large metal spoon

chef's knife

small knife   meat grinder

metal skewer

*cheesecloth can also be used

Stuffed cabbage is an old favorite. Here the leaves are blanched, then reassembled around a richly flavored stuffing. Served with a tomato-mushroom sauce, it makes a hearty main course.

SHOPPING LIST

1	medium head of Savoy cabbage, weighing 3 lb
For the chestnut stuffing	
2 lb	fresh chestnuts or 1 lb canned or vacuum-packed unsweetened chestnuts
4 oz	lean boneless pork
1	onion
1	lemon
10-12	sprigs of parsley
10-12	leaves of fresh sage
2	celery stalks
2	slices of white bread
1/4 cup	butter
	salt and pepper
2	eggs
For the tomato and mushroom sauce	
1 lb	tomatoes
1	small onion
4 oz	mushrooms
1	garlic clove
2 tbsp	vegetable oil
1 tbsp	tomato paste
1	bouquet garni made with 10-12 parsley stems, 2-3 thyme sprigs, and 1 bay leaf
	sugar

INGREDIENTS

Savoy cabbage

chestnuts   lean pork

lemon

onion

celery stalks

butter   white bread   vegetable oil

bouquet garni   tomato paste

sugar

mushrooms   fresh sage

garlic clove

eggs   tomatoes   parsley

ORDER OF WORK

1 PREPARE THE CABBAGE

2 MAKE THE CHESTNUT STUFFING

3 STUFF AND COOK THE CABBAGE

4 MAKE THE TOMATO AND MUSHROOM SAUCE

1 PREPARE THE CABBAGE

1 Using the small knife, cut the outside leaf from the base of the cabbage stem and carefully peel the leaf away from the head. Repeat until you have 10 large cabbage leaves. Wash the leaves well in cold water.

2 Bring a large saucepan of water to a boil. Add salt, then immerse the 10 cabbage leaves in the water and blanch 1 minute, just to soften them. With the slotted spoon, transfer the cabbage leaves to a bowl of cold water.

3 Trim the stem from the cabbage head and cook it in the boiling water, 3-4 minutes. Transfer it to a bowl of cold water. When cool, remove and let drain thoroughly, stem-end down, in the colander.

Outer leaves have deepest green color

Use small knife to cut out thick center rib

4 When the leaves are cool, drain and pat dry with paper towels. Cut out and discard the thick rib at the center of each large cabbage leaf.

5 Cut the cabbage head in half. Cut a wedge around the core in each piece of cabbage and remove it.

6 Set each half cut-side down on the chopping board and slice it crosswise into thin shreds. Discard any thick ribs. Roll up any loose leaves and cut them crosswise into shreds.

2 MAKE THE CHESTNUT STUFFING

1 If using fresh chestnuts, pierce each one with the point of the small knife. Put them in a pan with water to cover and bring to a boil. Remove a few chestnuts at a time and peel them with the knife while they are still hot.

If chestnuts become difficult to peel, return them to pan of water to reheat

2 Pour the water from the pan, return the peeled chestnuts to the pan, and cover with fresh water. Cover the pan with the lid and simmer until tender, 25-30 minutes. Drain well, then coarsely chop the chestnuts.

ANNE SAYS
"Canned and vacuum-packed chestnuts need not be cooked. Just drain them."

3 Cut the pork into 2-3 pieces and the onion into quarters. Work the pork and onion through the fine blade of the meat grinder or in the food processor.

4 Grate the zest from the lemon. Strip the parsley leaves from the sprigs and pile them on the chopping board with the sage leaves. With the chef's knife, finely chop the leaves.

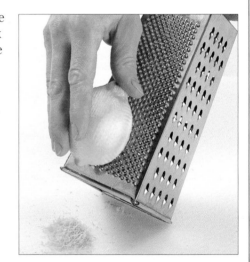

5 Peel the strings from the celery with the vegetable peeler and cut the stalks across into thin slices. Trim and discard the crusts from the slices of bread. Work the bread slices in the food processor, or in a blender, to form crumbs.

Celery slices neatly when strings have been removed

6 Melt the butter in the frying pan, add the shredded cabbage, and cook, stirring occasionally, until tender, 7-10 minutes. Transfer the cabbage to a large bowl, using the slotted spoon.

Add pork mixture all at once

7 Put the ground pork and onion into the frying pan with the celery. Cook, stirring occasionally, until the ground pork is crumbled and brown, 5-7 minutes.

8 Add the breadcrumbs, chestnuts, chopped herbs, lemon zest, salt, and pepper to the shredded cabbage in the bowl. Add the pork mixture and stir well together. Taste for seasoning.

9 Lightly beat the eggs with the fork. Pour the beaten egg into the stuffing mixture in the bowl and stir well together.

3 STUFF AND COOK THE CABBAGE

1 Line a large bowl with the dampened dish towel. Arrange 9 of the blanched cabbage leaves in an overlapping layer around the side of the bowl, stem-ends up. Allow about 2 inches of the leaves to extend above the rim of the bowl. Set the last leaf in the bottom of the bowl.

Arrange leaves to recreate original cabbage-head shape

2 Spoon in the chestnut stuffing, then press it down gently and smooth.

3 Fold the ends of the cabbage leaves over to enclose the chestnut stuffing completely.

4 Gather the ends of the cloth over the top of the cabbage leaves and tie them together with a piece of the string to make a tight ball.

5 Bring a large pan of water to a boil. Immerse the stuffed cabbage "head" in the water and set the heatproof plate on top to weigh it down.

6 Simmer until the skewer inserted in the center for 30 seconds comes out hot to the touch when removed, 50-60 minutes. Meanwhile, make the tomato and mushroom sauce.

4 MAKE THE TOMATO AND MUSHROOM SAUCE

1 Chop the tomatoes without peeling them. Peel the onion, leaving a little of the root attached, and cut it in half. Slice each half horizontally toward the root, leaving the slices attached at the root end. Slice vertically, again leaving the root end uncut. Cut across to make dice, then chop until very fine.

Tomato skin and seeds will be strained out later

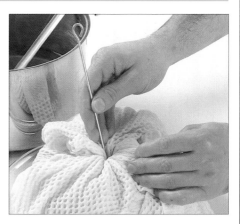

2 Wipe the mushrooms with a damp paper towel and trim the stems level with the caps. Set the mushrooms stem-side down on the chopping board and slice them. Set the flat side of the chef's knife on top of the garlic clove and strike it with your fist. Discard the skin and finely chop the clove.

3 Heat half of the vegetable oil in the frying pan. Add the chopped onion and cook, stirring with the wooden spoon, until soft, 2-3 minutes.

4 Stir in the tomatoes, tomato paste, garlic, bouquet garni, salt, pepper, and a pinch of sugar and cook, stirring occasionally, until the mixture is fairly thick, 8-10 minutes.

Straining removes bouquet garni as well as tomato skins and seeds

5 Strain the tomato mixture into a bowl, pressing down with the ladle to extract all the pulp.

6 Wipe the frying pan, heat the remaining oil, and sauté the mushrooms until tender, without letting them brown. Stir in the tomato sauce and taste for seasoning.

🍽 **TO SERVE**

Lift the stuffed "cabbage" carefully from the pan, drain, and let cool slightly. Unwrap and set it, stem-side down, on a warm serving plate. Spoon over some of the tomato and mushroom sauce and pass the rest separately. Cut into wedges to serve.

Fresh tomato and mushroom sauce is colorful contrasting accompaniment

Rich stuffing of chestnuts and pork is flavored with lemon and herbs

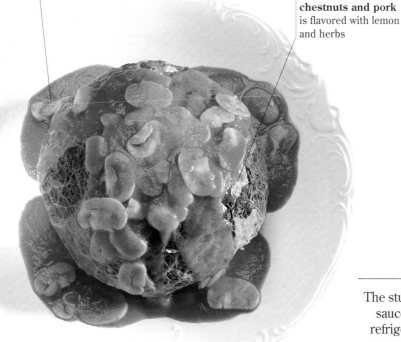

V A R I A T I O N

BABY GREEN CABBAGES STUFFED WITH PORK

Cured ham and pork fill the centers of these individual stuffed cabbages, served with sour cream or plain yogurt.

1 Prepare the cabbage as directed.
2 Make the stuffing as directed, omitting the chestnuts and using a total of 1 lb lean boneless pork.
3 Line 6 small bowls with pieces of cloth or cheesecloth. Add blanched cabbage leaves, using 2 leaves for each bowl.
4 Place 1 slice of cured ham on top of the cabbage in each bowl. Fill with the stuffing.
5 Tie up each stuffed cabbage "head" and cook as directed, allowing about 30 minutes.
6 Omit the tomato and mushroom sauce. Serve the baby green cabbages with sour cream or plain yogurt and decorate with fresh thyme.

──── **GETTING AHEAD** ────
The stuffed cabbage and tomato and mushroom sauce can be cooked 2 days ahead and kept refrigerated. Reheat the cabbage in a covered casserole with a little liquid in an oven heated to 350° F. Warm the sauce on top of the stove.

GRATIN OF ENDIVES AND HAM

🍽️ SERVES 4 🥄 WORK TIME 15-20 MINUTES 🍲 BAKING TIME 10-15 MINUTES

EQUIPMENT

saucepans, 1 with lid

small ladle

slotted spoon

strainer

2-pronged fork

plate

cheese grater

pastry brush

small knife

whisk

paper towels   quiche dish*

aluminum foil

chopping board

* shallow baking dish can also be used

INGREDIENTS

Belgian endives

Gruyère cheese

milk

sliced cooked ham

onion

sugar

ground nutmeg   bay leaf

flour

peppercorns   butter

In this simple dish from Belgium, home of endive, the endives are braised, wrapped with thin slices of cooked ham, and then baked in a cream sauce sprinkled with cheese.

GETTING AHEAD

The gratin can be assembled up to the baking stage, then covered tightly and refrigerated the day before baking.

SHOPPING LIST

	butter for quiche dish and foil
8	medium heads of Belgian endive, total weight about 2 lb
1 tsp	sugar
	salt and pepper
1½ oz	Gruyère cheese
8	thin slices of cooked ham, total weight about 12 oz
	For the béchamel sauce
2 cups	milk
1	slice of onion
1	bay leaf
6	peppercorns
¼ cup	butter
¼ cup	flour
	ground nutmeg

ORDER OF WORK

1 BRAISE ENDIVES

2 MAKE THE BÉCHAMEL SAUCE

3 ASSEMBLE AND BAKE THE GRATIN

1 BRAISE ENDIVES

1 Heat the oven to 350° F. Brush the quiche dish with butter. Trim the endives, wipe them with paper towels, and discard any wilted leaves.

Fresh endives are plump and white

2 With the point of the small knife, hollow each stem. If the endives are large, cut them in half.

ANNE SAYS
"This allows the endives to cook more evenly and removes the parts that may be bitter."

3 Arrange the endives in the prepared quiche dish and sprinkle with the sugar, salt, and pepper. Butter a piece of foil and press it buttered-side down, on top of the endives.

4 Bake the endives in the heated oven, turning once or twice with the 2-pronged fork, until they are brown and tender, 45-55 minutes. Using the slotted spoon, transfer the endives to the plate and let cool slightly. Wipe the quiche dish.

2 MAKE THE BECHAMEL SAUCE

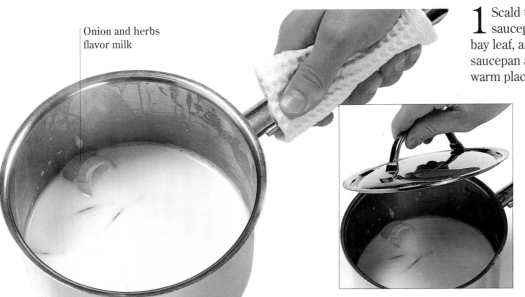

Onion and herbs flavor milk

1 Scald the milk in a medium saucepan with the onion slice, bay leaf, and peppercorns. Cover the saucepan and let the milk stand in a warm place, 10 minutes.

ANNE SAYS
"For a simple white sauce, omit the onion slice, bay leaf, and peppercorns and scald the milk"

Straining removes flavoring ingredients

2 Melt the butter in another saucepan over medium heat. Whisk in the flour and cook until foaming, 30-60 seconds.

3 Remove from the heat and let cool slightly, then strain in the hot milk and whisk to mix. Return to the heat and cook, whisking constantly, until the sauce boils and thickens. Season with salt, pepper, and a pinch of nutmeg, and simmer 2 minutes.

! TAKE CARE !
If the sauce forms lumps at any stage, remove from the heat and whisk vigorously. If whisking is not sufficient, strain the sauce.

3 ASSEMBLE AND BAKE THE GRATIN

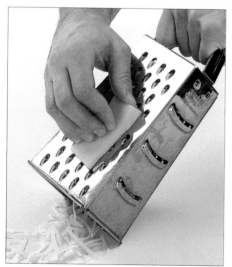

Centre endive on ham slice to roll up neatly

1 Heat the oven to 400° F. Butter the quiche dish again. Grate the Gruyère cheese and set aside.

2 Lay a slice of ham on the work surface. Set a head of endive on top and roll the ham slice round the endive to form a neat cylinder.

3 Repeat with the remaining ham slices and endives, arranging the cylinders neatly in the prepared dish, folded-side down, to keep them intact.

4 Ladle the béchamel sauce evenly over the endive and ham cylinders.

5 Sprinkle with the grated cheese. Bake in the heated oven until bubbling and browned, 20-25 minutes. If necessary, heat the broiler and broil the gratin until the top is brown. Serve hot from the quiche dish.

Gruyère cheese topping is brown and crisp

Endives are wrapped in tasty ham slices

V A R I A T I O N
BROCCOLI AND CAULIFLOWER GRATIN
This gratin is flavored with Parmesan cheese instead of ham.

1 Trim 1-2 heads of broccoli (total weight about 1 lb) and 1 head of cauliflower (weighing about 1½ lb). Cut the broccoli and cauliflower florets from the stems; cut large florets in half.
2 Bring 2 pans of water to a boil, add salt, and the broccoli and cauliflower florets to separate pans. Cook until just tender, 5-10 minutes. Drain thoroughly.
3 Arrange the florets in a buttered shallow baking dish, alternating the colors to make a checkerboard pattern.
4 Make the béchamel sauce as directed, adding ½ cup extra milk. Remove from the heat and whisk in 3 tbsp grated Parmesan cheese.
5 Spoon the sauce evenly over the florets and sprinkle with the grated Gruyère cheese. Bake as directed.

V A R I A T I O N
INDIVIDUAL GRATINS OF LEEK AND HAM
Leeks replace the Belgian endive in this gratin.

1 Trim 2 lb leeks, discarding the roots and tough tops. Cut off and reserve some of the tender green tops. Slit the leeks lengthwise and wash them thoroughly under cold running water.
2 Bring the leeks to a boil in a saucepan of water, add salt, and cook until tender, 12-20 minutes, depending on their size. Drain them, rinse with cold water, and drain again thoroughly. Cut the leeks into 5-inch lengths.
3 Cut the reserved green leek tops lengthwise in half, then cut lengthwise into thin strips to make julienne. Bring a pan of water to a boil, add salt, then the leek tops and cook until tender, 3-5 minutes. Drain and set aside.
4 Make the béchamel sauce as directed in the main recipe.
5 Heat the broiler. Cut the ham into strips 3-inches wide. Wrap the leek pieces in the ham strips so that the leeks show at each end. Arrange 3-4 on individual heatproof plates.
6 Spoon the sauce on top, omitting the grated cheese. Broil the gratins until browned, 3-5 minutes. Sprinkle the green leek julienne on the gratins just before serving.

ARTICHOKES STUFFED WITH MUSHROOMS AND OLIVES

Artichauts à la Barigoule

🍴 SERVES 4   🥣 WORK TIME 50-55 MINUTES   🍲 BAKING TIME 40-45 MINUTES

EQUIPMENT

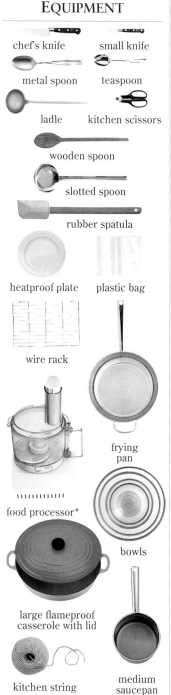

chef's knife

small knife

metal spoon

teaspoon

ladle

kitchen scissors

wooden spoon

slotted spoon

rubber spatula

heatproof plate

plastic bag

wire rack

frying pan

food processor*

bowls

large flameproof casserole with lid

kitchen string

medium saucepan

*blender can also be used

INGREDIENTS

globe artichokes

prosciutto

anchovy fillets

fresh thyme

mushrooms

onions

fresh basil

butter

black olives

olive oil

scallions

lemon

ground allspice

red bell peppers

white bread

tomatoes

garlic cloves

white wine

"A la barigoule" describes a Provençal method of preparing stuffed artichokes. Here, the artichokes are long-simmered with white wine and served with a rich red pepper sauce.

SHOPPING LIST

4	large globe artichokes, total weight about 3 lb
½	lemon
	salt and pepper
1 cup	white wine
For the mushroom and olive stuffing	
6	garlic cloves
3	small onions
8 oz	mushrooms
2-3	sprigs of fresh thyme
2	anchovy fillets
1 cup	pitted black olives
8 oz	prosciutto
4	slices of white bread
3 tbsp	butter
	ground allspice
For the red pepper sauce	
1½ lb	red bell peppers
1 lb	tomatoes
1	garlic clove
2	scallions
1	small bunch of fresh basil
2 tbsp	olive oil

ORDER OF WORK

1. **PREPARE THE ARTICHOKES**

2. **MAKE THE STUFFING**

3. **STUFF AND BAKE THE ARTICHOKES**

4. **MAKE THE RED PEPPER SAUCE**

1 PREPARE THE ARTICHOKES

1 Snap the stem from each artichoke so that the fibers are pulled out with the stem.

Grip stem firmly so it snaps sharply

2 Trim the base of each artichoke with the chef's knife so they sit flat, and rub the cut surfaces with the lemon half to prevent discoloration.

3 Trim the outer leaves from all the artichokes with the kitchen scissors to remove the pointed leaf tips.

4 With the chef's knife, cut off about ¾ inch from the pointed top of each artichoke. Rub all cut surfaces with lemon.

Keep artichokes submerged in water while they cook so they do not discolor

5 Fill the casserole with water, bring to a boil, and add salt. Remove from heat and add the artichokes. Weigh them down with the heatproof plate or a wet cloth to submerge them. Return to heat and simmer until almost tender and a leaf can be pulled out with a slight tug, 25-30 minutes. Set 1 artichoke on the wire rack to test.

ANNE SAYS
"Make the stuffing while the artichokes are cooking."

6 Lift out the artichokes with the slotted spoon and set them upside-down on the wire rack placed over the tray to drain.

7 When the artichokes are cool enough to handle, remove the inner leaves by twisting them out with your fingers.

When artichoke is fully cooked, choke is easy to remove

8 With the teaspoon, scoop out the choke from each to make a neat cavity for the stuffing.

2 MAKE THE STUFFING

1 Set the flat side of the chef's knife on top of each garlic clove and strike it with your fist. Discard the skin and finely chop the garlic. Peel the onions, leaving a little of the root attached to each, and cut them in half through root and stem. Slice each half horizontally toward the root, leaving the slices attached at the root end, then slice vertically, again leaving the root end uncut. Cut across the onion to make dice.

Slice just to root each time, so onion holds together

2 Wipe the mushroom caps with a damp paper towel and trim the stems. Cut the caps into quarters and coarsely chop them in the food processor, using the pulse button. Or, chop with the chef's knife.

3 Strip the thyme leaves from the stems and pile them on the chopping board. Finely chop the leaves. Chop the anchovy fillets. Finely chop the olives. Cut the prosciutto crosswise into thin strips.

Stack slices of prosciutto

4 Trim and discard the crusts from the bread. Work the bread slices in the food processor to form crumbs.

5 Melt the butter in the frying pan, add the chopped onions and garlic, and cook, stirring with the wooden spoon, until soft but not brown.

6 Stir in the mushrooms, prosciutto, anchovies, and olives, then remove the pan from the heat. Add the breadcrumbs, chopped thyme, and a large pinch of allspice and mix thoroughly. Season to taste with pepper.

3 STUFF AND BAKE THE ARTICHOKES

1 Heat the oven to 350°F. Spoon stuffing into the center of each artichoke to fill the cavity.

Mound stuffing well in artichokes

2 Tie a piece of kitchen string around each of the stuffed artichokes to hold the leaves together.

Wine will give flavor but alcohol is boiled away

String holds shape of artichokes as they simmer

3 Put the artichokes in the casserole and pour in the wine. Put the casserole over high heat, bring the wine to a boil, and boil until reduced by half, about 5 minutes. Pour in enough water to half cover the artichokes and add salt and pepper. Bring back to a boil and cover with the lid.

ANNE SAYS

"The casserole should be deep enough to hold the artichokes and large enough for them to fit snugly."

4 Transfer to the oven. Bake, basting occasionally, until tender and a central leaf can be pulled out easily, 40-50 minutes. Meanwhile, make the red pepper sauce.

ANNE SAYS

"Add more water during cooking if necessary to keep the artichokes moist."

4 MAKE THE RED PEPPER SAUCE

Steam trapped inside bag loosens skin

1 Heat the broiler. Set the bell peppers on a rack about 4 inches from the heat and broil, turning once or twice, until the skin is black and blistered. Put the peppers into the plastic bag, close, and let cool. Peel the peppers, using the small knife.

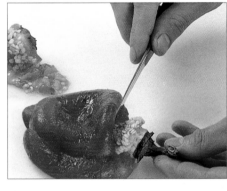

2 Rinse the peppers and pat them dry. Cut around the core and pull it out. Halve the peppers and scrape out the seeds. Cut the peppers into chunks.

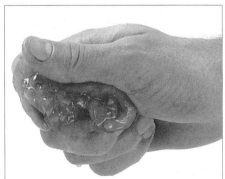

3 Score an "x" on the base of each tomato. Immerse them in boiling water until the skin starts to split. Transfer to cold water, then peel.

4 Cut the tomatoes in half and squeeze out the seeds. Chop the tomato halves.

5 Chop the garlic. Chop the scallions. Strip the basil leaves from the stems, reserving 4 sprigs for garnish, and finely chop the leaves.

6 Heat the olive oil in the frying pan. Add the bell peppers, tomatoes, garlic, scallions, and basil and cook, stirring occasionally, until thickened, 15-20 minutes.

7 Put the sauce in the food processor and purée until still slightly chunky in texture. Season the sauce to taste with salt and pepper.

Artichoke leaves can be pulled out one by one and dipped in red pepper sauce before tender bases are eaten

Basil sprig garnish echoes flavoring of red pepper sauce

¡⊙¡ TO SERVE
Discard the strings from the artichokes and put the artichokes on individual plates. Spoon some red pepper sauce around the base of each artichoke, garnish with a basil sprig, and pass the remaining sauce separately.

VARIATION

ARTICHOKES WITH HERB-BUTTER SAUCE

Artichokes, complemented by an herb-butter sauce, make an excellent dinner appetizer.

1 Prepare the artichokes as directed, cooking them for 35-45 minutes, until a central leaf can be pulled out easily. Drain upside-down and let cool slightly.
2 Meanwhile, make the sauce: Finely chop 2 shallots. Boil with 3 tbsp each white wine vinegar and white wine, until reduced to a glaze. Add 1 tbsp heavy cream and boil again to a glaze.
3 Take the pan from the heat and whisk in thoroughly 8 oz very cold butter, cut into cubes, a few pieces at a time. Move the pan on and off the heat so that the butter thickens and becomes creamy without melting to oil.
4 Over high heat bring the sauce just to a boil, whisking. Stir in 2 tbsp chopped mixed fresh herbs, salt, and pepper.
5 Remove the inner leaves and choke from each artichoke as directed. Spoon some of the sauce into the cup formed by the artichoke leaves and serve the rest separately. Decorate with a few herb sprigs.

GETTING AHEAD
The artichokes and red pepper sauce can be made 1 day ahead and kept refrigerated. Reheat both on top of the stove just before serving.

ORIENTAL DEEP-FRIED VEGETABLES

Tempura

 SERVES 6-8 WORK TIME 45-50 MINUTES  BAKING TIME 3-5 MINUTES EACH BATCH

EQUIPMENT

deep-fat fryer

2-pronged fork

small saucepan

deep-fat thermometer (if needed)

grater

baking sheets

chef's knife

small knife

whisk

bowls

vegetable peeler

wide slotted spoon

shallow dishes

strainer

chopping board   paper towels

Tempura was actually introduced into Japan by Portuguese missionaries as a way to cook fish. Today, an authentic version of these Japanese fritters is based on vegetables, though meat, poultry, or shellfish may be added.

INGREDIENTS

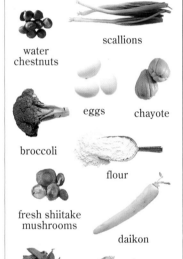

water chestnuts

scallions

eggs   chayote

broccoli

flour

fresh shiitake mushrooms

daikon

snow peas

sweet potatoes

fresh ginger root

oil for deep-frying   sake   light soy sauce

SHOPPING LIST

1	small head of broccoli, weighing about 8 oz
2	medium chayotes, total weight about 1 lb, or 2 small zucchini, total weight about 12 oz
4 oz	snow peas
8	scallions
2	sweet potatoes, total weight about 10 oz
8 oz	fresh shiitake mushrooms
4 oz	canned water chestnuts
	vegetable oil for deep-frying
1/2 cup	flour for dredging
	For the dipping sauce
2-oz	piece of daikon (white radish)
1-inch	piece of fresh ginger root
1/2 cup	sake
1/2 cup	light soy sauce
	For the batter
2 cups	flour
2	eggs
2 cups	cold water

ORDER OF WORK

1 **PREPARE THE VEGETABLES**

2 **MAKE THE DIPPING SAUCE**

3 **COAT AND DEEP-FRY THE VEGETABLES**

1 PREPARE THE VEGETABLES

1 Trim the head of broccoli, peeling the stem with the small knife to remove any tough fibers. Cut the broccoli florets from the stem where they begin to branch off, leaving about 2 inches of stem below the floret. Cut large florets in half.

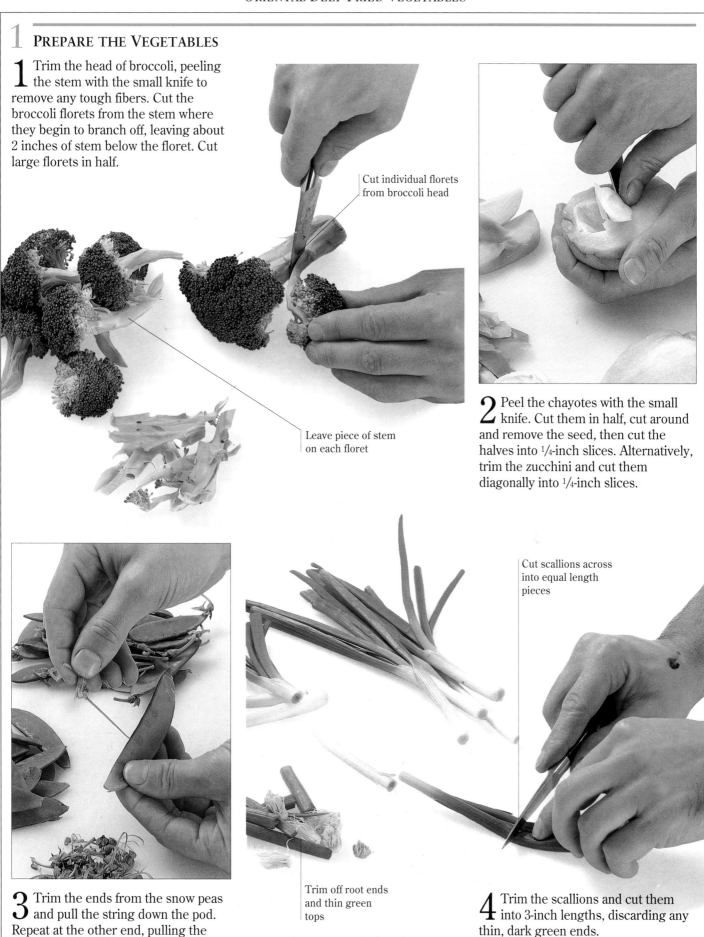

Cut individual florets from broccoli head

Leave piece of stem on each floret

2 Peel the chayotes with the small knife. Cut them in half, cut around and remove the seed, then cut the halves into ¼-inch slices. Alternatively, trim the zucchini and cut them diagonally into ¼-inch slices.

Cut scallions across into equal length pieces

3 Trim the ends from the snow peas and pull the string down the pod. Repeat at the other end, pulling the string from the other side.

Trim off root ends and thin green tops

4 Trim the scallions and cut them into 3-inch lengths, discarding any thin, dark green ends.

5 Using the vegetable peeler, peel the sweet potatoes, and halve them lengthwise. With the chef's knife cut the potato halves horizontally into ¼-inch slices.

6 Drain the water chestnuts and slice them thickly with the small knife.

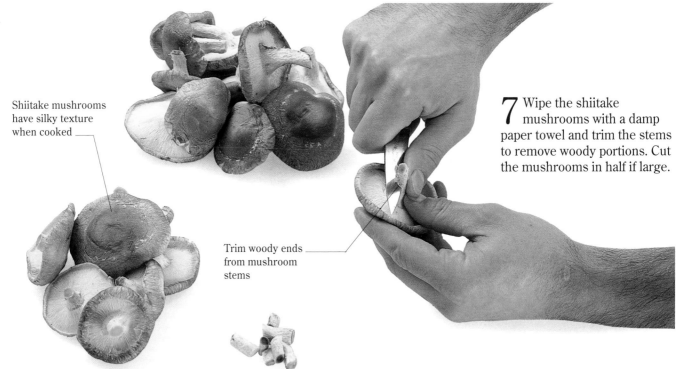

Shiitake mushrooms have silky texture when cooked

Trim woody ends from mushroom stems

7 Wipe the shiitake mushrooms with a damp paper towel and trim the stems to remove woody portions. Cut the mushrooms in half if large.

2 MAKE THE DIPPING SAUCE

1 Trim the end from the piece of daikon, if necessary, then peel it with the vegetable peeler. Grate the daikon.

Use large holes of grater to produce shreds of daikon

Hold grater firmly, at an angle

2 With the small knife, cut the skin from the ginger root. With the chef's knife, slice the ginger, cutting across the fibrous grain.

Rock blade of knife
to and fro

3 Crush each slice of ginger with the flat side of the chef's knife, then finely chop the slices.

4 Mix the sake and soy sauce together. Add the grated daikon and chopped ginger and set aside.

3 COAT AND DEEP-FRY THE VEGETABLES

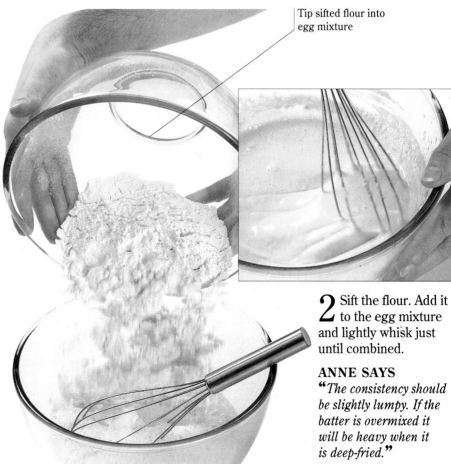

Tip sifted flour into
egg mixture

1 To make the batter: Lightly beat the eggs in a large bowl. Stir the water into the eggs, using the whisk.

2 Sift the flour. Add it to the egg mixture and lightly whisk just until combined.

ANNE SAYS
"The consistency should be slightly lumpy. If the batter is overmixed it will be heavy when it is deep-fried."

Toss broccoli in flour so pieces are lightly coated

3 Heat the oil in the deep-fat fryer until it is hot enough to brown a cube of fresh bread in 40 seconds. Heat the oven to very low.

ANNE SAYS
"If using a deep-fat thermometer, it should register 375°F."

4 Pour the batter into a large shallow dish. Put the flour for dredging in another shallow dish. Toss the broccoli florets and stems in the flour to coat lightly.

Let excess batter drip off before frying vegetables

5 Dip the vegetable pieces in the batter so they are completely coated. With the 2-pronged fork, lift out the florets, draining them 1-2 seconds to remove excess batter. Lower the pieces gently into the hot oil.

6 Deep-fry the broccoli florets until crisp, 3-5 minutes, turning once during cooking. With the slotted spoon transfer the broccoli to the baking sheet lined with several layers of paper towels. Keep warm in the oven.

! TAKE CARE !
It is important to deep-fry in small batches so the fryer is not crowded and the oil temperature remains constant.

7 Cook the other vegetables in the same way, flouring them, then coating with batter, deep-frying and transferring to lined baking sheets. Keep them warm in the oven until all are deep-fried.

! TAKE CARE !
Do not cover vegetables while keeping them warm.

Spread out deep-fried vegetables so coating remains crisp

Oriental sauce is pungent and spicy

TO SERVE
Arrange the deep-fried vegetables on a serving platter. Warm the dipping sauce in the saucepan just until hot, and taste for seasoning. Serve it separately for dipping.

VARIATION
FRITTO MISTO

1 Omit the dipping sauce. Prepare the scallions and sweet potatoes, as directed in the main recipe.

2 Trim the florets from 1 medium head of cauliflower, cutting large florets in half or into quarters.

3 Prepare 8 oz cultivated mushrooms: Wipe the caps with a damp paper towel and trim the stems even with the caps; cut the caps in half if they are large.

4 Peel 8 oz asparagus, using the vegetable peeler to strip away the tough outer skin at the bottom of each asparagus spear. Cut the spears into 3-inch lengths. Blanch in boiling salted water for 3 minutes, drain, rinse with cold water, and drain well again.

5 Cut 8 oz mozzarella into sticks about 3 inches long. Cut 3-4 lemons into wedges for serving.

6 Lightly flour the vegetables and cheese. Dip the mushrooms and cheese into 2 lightly beaten eggs, then coat with 1 cup dry breadcrumbs seasoned with salt and pepper.

7 Deep-fry the coated mushrooms and cheese 3-5 minutes; drain and keep warm. Prepare the batter. Dip the remaining vegetables in batter and deep-fry them as directed.

8 Arrange the cheese and vegetables on individual plates with wedges of lemon for squeezing.

GETTING AHEAD
The vegetables and ingredients for the sauce can be prepared up to 2 hours ahead. Make the batter and deep-fry the vegetables just before serving.

Swiss Chard Crepes with Three Cheeses

 SERVES 6   WORK TIME 1 HOUR*   BAKING TIME 20-25 MINUTES

EQUIPMENT

- bowls
- cheese grater
- vegetable peeler
- small knife
- plate
- chef's knife
- small ladle
- metal spoon
- whisk
- metal spatula
- large frying pan
- teaspoon
- colander
- 8-inch crêpe pan*
- saucepans
- wooden spoon
- shallow baking dish
- strainer

*flat-bottomed frying pan can also be used

Thin, lacy crêpes are filled with a vigorous combination of Swiss chard, goat cheese, feta, chopped shallots, and garlic, then topped with a light cream sauce. Napa or Chinese cabbage can be substituted for the chard.

* plus 30-60 minutes standing time

SHOPPING LIST

	butter for baking dish
For the crêpe batter	
1 cup	flour
¹⁄₂ tsp	salt
3	eggs
1 cup	milk
3-4 tbsp	vegetable oil
For the Swiss chard and cheese filling	
1¹⁄₂ lb	Swiss chard
3	shallots
2	garlic cloves
2 tbsp	butter
¹⁄₃ cup	soft goat cheese
¹⁄₂ cup	fresh feta cheese
	salt and pepper
	ground nutmeg
For the white cream sauce	
1 cup	milk
2 tbsp	butter
2 tbsp	flour
¹⁄₂ cup	heavy cream
	ground nutmeg
1 oz	Gruyère cheese for sprinkling

INGREDIENTS

- Swiss chard
- garlic cloves
- shallots
- Gruyère cheese
- feta cheese
- soft goat cheese
- milk
- ground nutmeg
- eggs
- butter
- heavy cream
- flour
- vegetable oil

ORDER OF WORK

1. MAKE THE CREPES

2. PREPARE THE SWISS CHARD

3. MAKE THE FILLING

4. FILL AND BAKE THE CREPES

1 MAKE THE CREPES

1 Sift the flour and salt into a medium bowl and make a well in the center. Pour the eggs into the well and whisk just until mixed.

2 Add half of the milk and whisk, drawing in the flour to make a paste. Stir in half of the remaining milk. Cover and let stand 30-60 minutes. Meanwhile, prepare the Swiss chard and make the filling (see pages 98-99).

3 After the batter has been standing, stir the remaining milk into the batter, adding enough so it is the consistency of thin cream.

Batter that has been left to stand will make light crêpes, because starch in flour has expanded

Bubbles around edge show crêpe pan is hot

4 To fry the crêpes: Heat about 1 tbsp oil in the crêpe pan until very hot; pour off the excess, reserving it to grease the pan. Add a drop of batter and wait until it sputters, showing the pan is hot. Pour in a small ladle of batter, shaking the pan to coat the bottom evenly with batter.

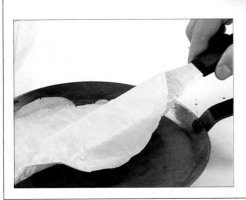

5 Fry the crêpe quickly over medium heat until it is set on top and brown underneath, 1-2 minutes. Loosen the crêpe, then turn or flip it over with the help of the metal spatula, and continue cooking the crêpe until it is brown on the other side, 30-60 seconds.

6 Transfer the crêpe to the plate. Continue making crêpes, adding oil to the pan as necessary, until all the batter is used, to make a total of 12 crêpes. Pile them on the plate so that they stay moist and warm.

2 PREPARE THE SWISS CHARD

1 With the chef's knife trim off the root from the Swiss chard and discard any tough stems and leaves. Thoroughly wash the stems and leaves.

2 Cut off the green tops from around the stems and set the green tops aside. Using the vegetable peeler, remove any strings from the outer sides of the stems.

Green tops of chard are cooked separately from stems at this stage

Slice chard stems in thick chunks

3 Cut the stems into ³/₈-inch slices and reserve them. Bring a large pan of water to a boil, add salt, and the green tops, and simmer until tender, 2-3 minutes. Drain in the colander, rinse with cold water, and drain again thoroughly. Chop the tops with the chef's knife.

3 MAKE THE FILLING

1 Chop the shallots (see box, page 99). Set the flat side of the chef's knife on top of the garlic cloves and strike it with your fist. Discard the skin and finely chop the cloves.

Diced shallot adds flavor to filling

Chop garlic finely by rocking knife blade up and down

2 Heat the butter in the large frying pan. Add the garlic and shallots and cook until soft but not brown, 1-2 minutes. Add the sliced chard stems and sauté, stirring, until just tender, 3-5 minutes.

Add green chard tops when stems are tender

3 Add the chopped Swiss chard tops and sauté, stirring, until all moisture has evaporated, 2-3 minutes. Remove the pan from the heat.

4 Crumble the goat cheese into the sautéed Swiss chard mixture, then crumble in the feta cheese. Season to taste with salt, pepper, and a pinch of nutmeg. Stir to mix, then set aside while making the crêpes.

Crumble cheese with fingers

HOW TO CHOP A SHALLOT

For a standard chop, make slices that are about ⅛-inch thick. For a fine chop, make the slices as thin as possible.

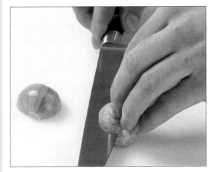

1 Peel the outer papery skin from the shallot. Separate into sections at the root, peel if necessary, and halve. Set each section flat-side down on a chopping board, hold steady with your fingers and slice horizontally, leaving the slices attached at the root end.

2 Slice vertically through the shallot, again leaving the root end uncut.

3 Cut across the shallot to make fine dice. Continue chopping until the dice are very fine.

4 FILL AND BAKE THE CREPES

Press cheese
against grater
with fingertips

1 Heat the oven to 350°F. Butter the baking dish. To make the white cream sauce: Scald the milk in a saucepan. Melt the butter in another saucepan over medium heat. Whisk in the flour and cook until foaming, 30-60 seconds.

2 Remove from the heat and let cool slightly, then whisk in the hot milk. Return to the heat and cook, whisking constantly, until the sauce boils and thickens. Whisk in the cream. Season with salt, pepper, and a pinch of nutmeg ; simmer 2 minutes. Remove from the heat, cover, and keep warm.

3 Grate the Gruyère cheese, holding it with your fingertips.

4 Put 2 spoonfuls of filling onto one half of the paler side of a crêpe.

Baking dish is
buttered to keep
crêpes from sticking

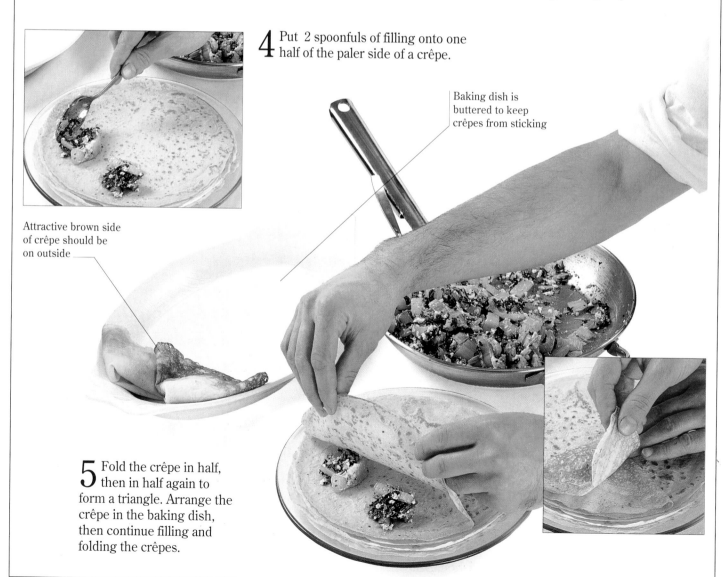

Attractive brown side
of crêpe should be
on outside

5 Fold the crêpe in half, then in half again to form a triangle. Arrange the crêpe in the baking dish, then continue filling and folding the crêpes.

6 Repeat until all the crêpes are used, overlapping them in the dish until it is full.

Overlap crêpes to keep them moist

7 If necessary, reheat the sauce, stirring until smooth. Spoon the sauce over the crêpes to coat them completely. Sprinkle with the grated Gruyère cheese. Bake in the heated oven until the sauce is bubbling and brown, 20-25 minutes. Serve hot from the baking dish.

Gruyère cheese gives attractive golden brown top to dish

Crêpes enclose a rich cheese and Swiss chard mixture

GETTING AHEAD
The crêpes can be prepared, filled, and kept up to 3 days in the refrigerator. They can also be frozen. Bake them just before serving.

VARIATION

CREPES WITH WILD MUSHROOMS AND HERBS

Here crêpes are rolled around a succulent filling of wild and cultivated mushrooms.

1 Make the crêpes as directed.
2 Wipe 8 oz fresh shiitake, or other wild mushrooms with a damp paper towel, trim the stems and halve any large mushrooms. Cut the mushrooms into 1/2-inch slices. (Alternatively, soak 1 1/2 oz dried wild mushrooms in warm water until plump, about 30 minutes, then drain, and continue as for fresh mushrooms.) Clean 8 oz common mushrooms, trim stems even with caps, then with stem-sides down, slice.
3 Melt the butter, add the chopped garlic, shallots, and wild and cultivated mushrooms, and sauté until the liquid has evaporated, stirring constantly, about 5 minutes. Set aside a few sautéed mushrooms for garnish.
4 Strip the leaves from several sprigs of fresh herbs such as parsley, tarragon, and chives. Chop the leaves.
5 Make the white sauce as directed, saving the cream to add later, then stir in the herbs. Mix half of the herb sauce with the mushrooms, put mixture in the middle of each crêpe, fold in 2 sides, and roll up into cylinders. Arrange in a buttered baking dish.
6 Add the cream to the remaining herb sauce and pour it over the crêpes. Bake as directed, omitting the grated cheese. Garnish with the reserved mushrooms just before serving.

CHEESE-STUFFED GREEN BELL PEPPERS

🍴 SERVES 4　🥄 WORK TIME 30-35 MINUTES*　🍲 BAKING TIME 45-50 MINUTES

EQUIPMENT

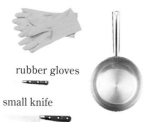

rubber gloves

small knife

chef's knife

metal spoon

frying pan

teaspoon

slotted spoon

citrus juicer

baking dish

bowls

paper towels

whisk

large metal spoon

metal spatula

saucepan

cheese grater

wooden spoon

chopping board

plastic bags

In this version of the Mexican dish Chiles Rellenos, green bell peppers stuffed with cheese and onions are baked in a light custard. Poblano chilis are traditional for stuffing because of their mild flavor and large size, so use them if you can find them.

* plus 30 minutes standing time

INGREDIENTS

fresh hot chili peppers

garlic cloves

onions

mild Cheddar cheese**

eggs

tomatoes

fresh coriander

milk

vegetable oil

Tabasco sauce

dried oregano

green bell peppers

lemon juice

**Monterey Jack cheese can also be used

SHOPPING LIST

8	large green bell peppers, total weight about 2 lb
2	medium onions
2 tbsp	vegetable oil, more for baking dish
1 lb	mild Cheddar cheese
2 tsp	dried oregano
	salt and pepper
For the tomato salsa	
2	garlic cloves
2	large onions
1 lb	tomatoes
1	small bunch of fresh coriander (cilantro)
2	fresh hot chili peppers
	juice of 1 lemon
1 tsp	Tabasco sauce
For the custard	
3	eggs
½ cup	milk
½ tsp	dried oregano

ORDER OF WORK

1 MAKE THE TOMATO SALSA

2 ROAST AND PEEL THE BELL PEPPERS

3 STUFF THE BELL PEPPERS

4 BAKE THE BELL PEPPERS

1 MAKE THE TOMATO SALSA

1 Finely chop the garlic. Chop the onions. Peel, seed, and finely chop the tomatoes (see box, below). Strip the coriander leaves from the stems and pile them on the chopping board. Finely chop the leaves.

2 Wearing the rubber gloves, cut the chili peppers in half lengthwise; discard the core. Scrape out the seeds, cut away the fleshy white ribs, then cut into thin strips. Lay them together and cut across to make very fine dice.

3 Mix the chopped tomatoes, garlic, onions, chili peppers, lemon juice, coriander, and Tabasco sauce and season to taste with salt. Let stand at least 30 minutes.

HOW TO PEEL, SEED, AND CHOP TOMATOES

Tomatoes are often peeled and seeded before chopping so they will cook to form a smooth purée.

1 Bring a small saucepan of water to a boil. Using a small knife, cut out the cores from the tomatoes. Score an "x" on the base of each tomato with the tip of the knife.

"x" on base of tomato will let skin split

2 Immerse the tomatoes in the water and boil until the skin starts to split, 8-15 seconds, depending on their ripeness. Transfer them at once to a bowl of cold water to stop the cooking.

3 Peel the skin from the tomatoes with the help of a small knife. Cut the tomatoes crosswise in half and squeeze out the seeds.

4 Set each half cut-side down on the chopping board and slice. Give the slices a half turn and slice again. Chop the flesh coarsely or finely, as needed.

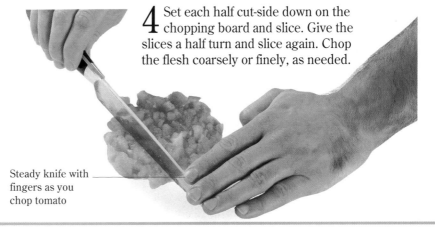

Steady knife with fingers as you chop tomato

2 ROAST AND PEEL THE BELL PEPPERS

Loosened skin peels off easily

1 Heat the broiler and set the whole bell peppers on a rack about 4 inches from the heat. Broil them, turning once or twice, until the skin is black and blistered, 10-12 minutes. Wrap in the plastic bags and let cool.

ANNE SAYS
"The steam trapped inside the plastic bag helps loosen the skin."

2 With the small knife, peel off the skin from each bell pepper, then rinse the peeled peppers under cold running water. Pat them dry with paper towels.

3 Cut out the core from the center of each pepper, then scrape out the seeds with the teaspoon and discard them.

3 STUFF THE BELL PEPPERS

Pack stuffing into peppers

1 Chop the onions. Heat the vegetable oil in the frying pan, add the onions and cook, stirring, until soft but not brown. Let cool. Grate the cheese and put it in a bowl. Add the oregano, salt, pepper, and sautéed onions and mix together. Taste the stuffing for seasoning.

2 Oil the baking dish. Spoon the cheese-onion mixture into each prepared bell pepper and put the peppers sideways in the dish.

ANNE SAYS
"The stuffed peppers should fit snugly in the baking dish."

4 BAKE THE BELL PEPPERS

1 Heat the oven to 350° F.
Make the custard:
Whisk together the eggs,
milk, oregano, salt, and
pepper. Pour the custard
around the peppers.

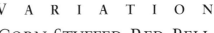

Pour herbed custard
into baking dish

Peppers are plump
when filled

2 Bake in the heated oven,
45-50 minutes; test whether the
custard is set with the point of a knife.

🍽️ TO SERVE
Decorate the tomato salsa with fresh
coriander leaves and serve with the
hot stuffed peppers.

Custard puffs
appetizingly
around baked
peppers

VARIATION

CORN-STUFFED RED BELL PEPPERS

*Red bell peppers, stuffed with
corn and cheese, make a pretty
presentation.*

1 Cook 2 ears of corn in a large pan of
boiling water until the kernels pop out
easily when tested with the point of a
knife, 5-7 minutes. Drain the corn and
cut the corn kernels from the cob.
Alternatively, thaw 1 cup frozen corn
kernels, or use an equal amount of
drained canned corn.
2 Make the tomato salsa as directed.
3 Peel, core, and seed 8 red bell
peppers as directed.
4 Make the cheese filling as
directed and stir in the corn
kernels. Stuff the peppers
and arrange upright in
individual baking dishes,
2 peppers to each dish.
5 Pour in the custard and
bake as directed.

Piquant salsa makes
good accompaniment
to baked peppers

GETTING AHEAD
The bell peppers can be stuffed and the
tomato salsa made up to 24 hours ahead and
refrigerated. Make the custard and bake the
peppers just before serving.

STIR-FRIED THAI VEGETABLES

🍽 SERVES 4 🥣 WORK TIME 30-35 MINUTES ♨ COOKING TIME 15-20 MINUTES

EQUIPMENT

chef's knife

small knife

fork

whisk

aluminum foil

colander

bowls

baking sheet

large saucepan

chopping board

pastry brush

baking dish

wok with stirrer*

*large frying pan can also be used

Almost any crisp vegetable is excellent stir-fried; this cooking method keeps the textures of the vegetables firm and the colors vivid.

GETTING AHEAD

Last-minute cooking is essential for a stir-fry. However, the vegetables can be prepared up to 2 hours ahead. The rice can also be cooked ahead and reheated in a low oven.

SHOPPING LIST

1½ cups	long-grain rice
	salt
1 oz	dried oriental mushrooms, or other dried wild mushrooms
1 cup	warm water, more if needed
½ cup	shelled, skinned raw peanuts
	butter for dish and foil
1	medium head of cauliflower, weighing about 1 lb
1 lb	bok choy, about 4 small heads
6 oz	snow peas
2	garlic cloves
1	medium red bell pepper
3-5	sprigs of fresh basil
6 oz	bean sprouts
1	stalk of lemon grass or 1 lemon
3 tbsp	fish sauce (nam pla)
2 tbsp	oyster sauce
1 tsp	cornstarch
1 tsp	sugar
3 tbsp	vegetable oil
2	dried hot red chili peppers

INGREDIENTS

dried oriental mushrooms

cauliflower

garlic cloves

fresh basil

lemon grass

raw peanuts

cornstarch

long-grain rice

vegetable oil

snow peas

bean sprouts

sugar

red bell pepper

dried hot red chili peppers

bok choy

fish sauce

oyster sauce

ORDER OF WORK

1 BOIL THE RICE

2 PREPARE THE VEGETABLES

3 STIR-FRY THE VEGETABLES

106

1 BOIL THE RICE

1 Cook the long-grain rice in boiling salted water until barely tender, 10-12 minutes. Meanwhile, soak the dried mushrooms and toast the peanuts (see Prepare the Vegetables, steps 1 and 2, below).

2 Drain the rice in the colander, rinse with cold running water to wash away the starch, and let drain thoroughly. Using the pastry brush, butter the baking dish and enough foil to cover the dish.

3 Spread the cooked rice evenly in the buttered baking dish, using the fork to fluff up the grains, and cover the dish with the buttered foil. Keep warm in the oven, turned to its lowest setting, after toasting the peanuts.

2 PREPARE THE VEGETABLES

1 Heat the oven to 375° F. Put the dried mushrooms in a bowl, pour over warm water to cover, and set the mushrooms aside to soften, about 30 minutes.

2 Meanwhile, spread the peanuts on the baking sheet and toast them in the oven until brown, 5-7 minutes. Coarsely chop them.

3 Trim the head of cauliflower to remove the outer green leaves. With the small knife, cut off the florets, discarding the stems.

4 Trim the stems of the bok choy. Cut each head lengthwise in half. Pile the halves 2-3 at a time on the chopping board and slice them crosswise into shreds.

Hold bok choy firmly when slicing

5 Trim the ends from the snow peas and pull the string down the pod. Repeat at the other end, pulling the string from the other side.

6 Drain the mushrooms and slice them. Set the flat side of the chef's knife on top of the garlic cloves and strike it with your fist. Skin and finely chop the garlic cloves.

Rinse bean sprouts with cold water

7 With a sharp movement, twist the core out of the bell pepper, then halve the pepper and scrape out the seeds. Cut away the white ribs on the inside. Set each pepper half on the chopping board, flatten it, and slice it lengthwise into strips. Remove the basil leaves from the stems.

8 Rinse the bean sprouts in the colander. Trim the lemon grass. Slice the stalk lengthwise in half if it is large, then cut across to chop it. Alternatively, grate the zest from the lemon.

3 STIR-FRY THE VEGETABLES

2 Heat the oil in the wok. Add the chopped garlic and dried hot red chili peppers and stir-fry until the garlic is fragrant, 30 seconds. Add the cauliflower, red bell pepper, bean sprouts, and bok choy and cook, stirring constantly, until beginning to soften, 3-5 minutes.

Bok choy will wilt and lose volume

1 Put the fish sauce, oyster sauce, cornstarch, sugar, and chopped lemon grass in a small bowl, and whisk them together.

Lift and turn vegetables as they fry

3 Stir the mushrooms and snow peas into the vegetables in the wok and cook, stirring, 3 minutes.

4 Add the basil leaves and fish sauce mixture to the vegetables in the wok, and stir-fry 2 minutes longer. Taste and season with more fish sauce, oyster sauce, and sugar, if needed. Remove the chili peppers from the wok and discard.

ANNE SAYS
"As the mixture cooks, the cornstarch will slightly thicken the sauce."

🍴 TO SERVE
Make a ring of rice on a warmed plate. Spoon the vegetables and sauce into the center, and sprinkle with the chopped peanuts. If you like, pull out a few red bell pepper strips and arrange them decoratively on the rice.

Chopped toasted peanuts give crunchy texture

Bell pepper strips are bright garnish on rice

CHINESE STIR-FRIED VEGETABLES

This vegetable stir-fry is best served with boiled Chinese noodles.

1 Prepare the Chinese mushrooms, bok choy, and bean sprouts as directed; omit the cauliflower, snow peas, and red bell pepper.

2 Omit the peanuts; toast ½ cup sliced almonds in the oven, 3-5 minutes.

3 Prepare 1 medium head of broccoli: Trim the head, leaving about 2 inches of the stem. Strip the tough outer skin from the stem. Cut off the florets and cut the stem into 3-inch sticks.

4 Drain ½ cup canned bamboo shoots and ½ cup canned baby corn. Slice the green parts of 2 scallions.

5 Omit the fish sauce mixture. Whisk together 3 tbsp rice wine or dry sherry, 2 tbsp soy sauce, 2 tsp sesame oil, 1 tsp cornstarch, and a pinch of sugar.

6 Heat the oil in the wok, add the broccoli and bok choy, and stir-fry, 2-3 minutes. Add the mushrooms and baby corn and stir-fry 2 minutes.

7 Add the soy sauce mixture, bamboo shoots, bean sprouts, and scallions, and cook, stirring, 2 minutes. Season with more rice wine, soy sauce, sesame oil, and sugar, if needed, and sprinkle with the toasted sliced almonds.

MIXED VEGETABLE CURRY

Sabzi Kari

🍽 SERVES 6-8   🥣 WORK TIME 40-45 MINUTES   🍲 BAKING TIME 25-35 MINUTES

EQUIPMENT

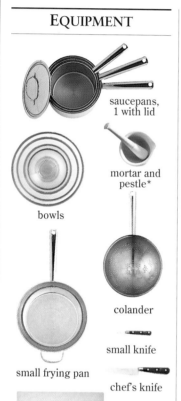

saucepans, 1 with lid

mortar and pestle*

bowls

colander

small knife

small frying pan

chef's knife

chopping board

strainer

wooden spoon

slotted spoon

large metal spoon

thin dish towel**

sauté pan with lid***

vegetable peeler

kitchen fork

*spice mill can also be used

**cheesecloth can also be used

***frying pan with lid can also be used

This vegetable curry is flavored with an exotic blend of spices and served with basmati rice. Chutney and a "raita" of diced cucumber and plain yogurt are also excellent accompaniments.

SHOPPING LIST

2 cups	basmati rice
6 1/2 cups	water
1 1/2 cups	unsweetened shredded coconut
	salt
	For the curry spice mixture
6	dried hot red chili peppers
12	cardamom pods
3 tbsp	coriander seeds
1 tbsp	cumin seeds
1/2 tsp	mustard seeds
2 tsp each	fenugreek seeds, ground turmeric and ginger
	For the vegetable stew
3	garlic cloves
4 each	medium onions, potatoes, and carrots (total weight about 2 3/4 lb)
1	small head of cauliflower, weighing about 2 lb
1 lb	green beans
4	large tomatoes, total weight about 1 1/2 lb
1/3 cup	vegetable oil
1	cinnamon stick
6	whole cloves
1 1/2 cups	shelled fresh or defrosted green peas

INGREDIENTS

basmati rice

dried hot red chili peppers

cinnamon stick

seeds

ground spices

cardamom pods

vegetable oil

cloves

potatoes

carrots

cauliflower

green peas

onions

garlic cloves

green beans

unsweetened shredded coconut

tomatoes

ORDER OF WORK

1 MAKE THE CURRY SPICE MIXTURE

2 PREPARE THE COCONUT MILK AND VEGETABLES

3 MAKE THE VEGETABLE CURRY

4 COOK THE BASMATI RICE

1 MAKE THE CURRY SPICE MIXTURE

1 Trim and split the dried hot red chili peppers. Using the small knife scrape out the seeds, then discard them.

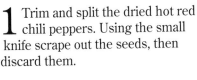

Scrape out seeds with small knife

2 Crush the cardamom pods in the mortar with the pestle and discard the pods, keeping the cardamom seeds in the mortar.

ANNE SAYS
"You can also use the end of a rolling pin to crush the cardamom pods."

Ready-ground spices are added to those prepared by hand

3 Put the chili peppers in the small frying pan with the coriander seeds and cumin seeds and toast the spices over medium heat, stirring constantly to prevent burning, until they are browned and very fragrant, about 2 minutes. Set aside to cool.

ANNE SAYS
"For toasting the spices, the pan should be dry, with no fat."

4 Put the toasted spices in the mortar with the cardamom seeds and add the mustard seeds and fenugreek seeds. Crush them to a fine powder.

ANNE SAYS
"The curry spice mixture can be kept up to a month in an airtight jar."

5 Add the turmeric and ginger, and stir the spices well to mix.

HOW TO MAKE COCONUT MILK

Not the same as the liquid inside a coconut, coconut "milk" is made by steeping shredded coconut in water.

1 Bring the water to a boil in a small saucepan. Add the shredded coconut and stir with the wooden spoon to mix, then cover and remove from heat. Let stand about 30 minutes.

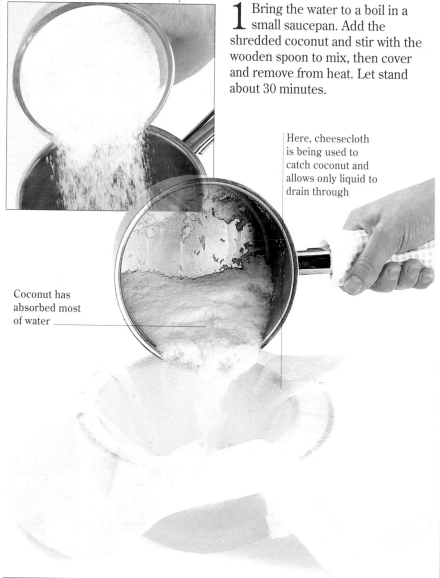

Here, cheesecloth is being used to catch coconut and allows only liquid to drain through

Coconut has absorbed most of water

2 Put a dish towel or a piece of cheesecloth in a strainer set in a bowl and pour in the shredded coconut and its liquid.

3 Gather up the ends of the cloth and squeeze the shredded coconut well to extract as much liquid or "milk" as possible. Discard the shredded coconut.

2 PREPARE THE COCONUT MILK AND VEGETABLES

1 Make coconut milk (see box, left), using 3 cups of the water and the coconut. Set the flat side of the chef's knife on top of each garlic clove and strike it with your fist. Discard the skin and finely chop the garlic.

2 Peel the onions, leaving a little of the roots attached, and cut them in half. Slice each half horizontally toward the root, then slice vertically, again leaving the root end uncut. Finally, cut across the onion to make dice.

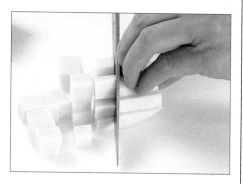

3 Peel the potatoes and square off the sides. Cut each one vertically into ½-inch slices, then stack the slices and cut into ½-inch strips. Cut across to make ½-inch dice. Put in a bowl of water so they do not discolor.

4 Trim the florets from the cauliflower stem and leaves. Cut the florets into small pieces.

Cauliflower florets need not be cut in even-sized pieces

Florets make crunchy curry ingredient

5 Peel the carrots, then roll-cut them: Cut a diagonal slice near the end of 1 carrot. Turn the carrot a quarter turn and make another diagonal cut in it. Continue to turn and cut all the carrot; repeat with the remaining carrots.

6 Snap off the ends of the green beans and cut them into 2-inch pieces.

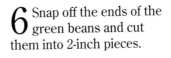

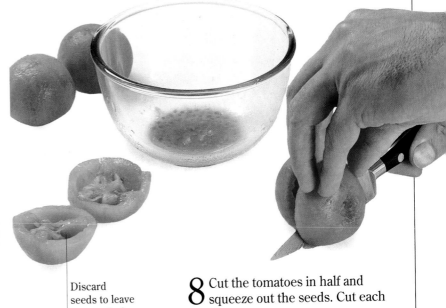

7 Score an "x" on the base of each tomato. Immerse in boiling water until the skin starts to split, 8-15 seconds. Transfer to a bowl of cold water. When cold, peel off the skin.

Discard seeds to leave tomato flesh

8 Cut the tomatoes in half and squeeze out the seeds. Cut each half into quarters.

3 **MAKE THE VEGETABLE CURRY**

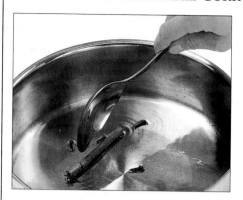

1 Heat the oil in the sauté pan, add the cinnamon stick and cloves, and cook until fragrant, 30-60 seconds.

2 Add the onions and garlic to the pan and sauté quickly, stirring to soften and cook evenly, until beginning to color.

Each vegetable adds different texture

3 Add the curry spice mixture and cook over low heat, stirring constantly, about 2-3 minutes.

Fresh or frozen green peas are good in curry

4 Drain the potatoes and add to the pan with the carrots, cauliflower, green beans, tomatoes, green peas, and salt to taste. Sauté, stirring occasionally, until thoroughly coated with spices, 3-5 minutes.

5 Add the coconut milk to the vegetables and stir together. Cover the pan and simmer until the vegetables are tender and the sauce is thick and rich, 15-20 minutes. Meanwhile, cook the basmati rice.

Coconut milk adds exotic flavor

Spices coat vegetables and give delicious aroma

6 Remove the cloves and cinnamon stick from the pan and discard. Taste the curry for seasoning.

4 COOK THE BASMATI RICE

1 Put the basmati rice in a large bowl, cover generously with cold water, and let soak 2-3 minutes, stirring occasionally. Drain the rice in the colander, rinse with cold water, and drain again thoroughly.

2 Put the drained rice in a saucepan with the remaining 3 ½ cups water and a pinch of salt. Bring to a boil, then cover the pan and simmer until the rice is just tender to the bite (al dente), 10-12 minutes. Remove from heat and leave covered for at least 5 minutes, then gently stir the rice to fluff it.

ANNE SAYS
"Do not remove the lid until just before serving, so that the rice will remain warm and fluffy."

TO SERVE
Divide the rice among warmed plates, spoon the vegetable curry next to it, and serve hot.

Vegetables and rice make dramatic presentation when served in this way

VARIATION
WINTER VEGETABLE CURRY
Mixed Vegetable Curry takes a seasonal turn with a selection of winter vegetables.

1 Prepare the curry spice mixture, coconut milk, onions, garlic, potatoes, carrots, and cauliflower as directed in the main recipe; omit the green beans, tomatoes, and peas.
2 Discard the seeds from a 1-lb piece of pumpkin, cut it into 3-inch pieces, and peel the skin from them with a small knife. Dice the flesh.
3 Trim, peel and dice 3 medium turnips (total weight about 12 oz). Trim 8 oz Brussels sprouts.
4 Sauté the onions and garlic with the curry spice mixture. Add the prepared vegetables and continue with the curry as directed in the main recipe, simmering it 15-20 minutes.
5 Spread the rice in a large, shallow serving bowl. Spoon out a few of the Brussels sprouts to arrange on the rice. Mold the curry in a bowl: Oil a deep soup bowl, fill it with curry, and press down lightly. Leave 1 minute, then turn out onto the rice. For a quicker serving, make a well in the center and add the vegetable curry. Serve hot.

GETTING AHEAD
The vegetable curry can be made up to 3 days in advance and refrigerated; the flavor will mellow. The basmati rice is best cooked just before serving.

EGGPLANT CANNELLONI

🍽 SERVES 4-6   🥣 WORK TIME 40-45 MINUTES*   ♨ COOKING TIME 70-75 MINUTES

EQUIPMENT

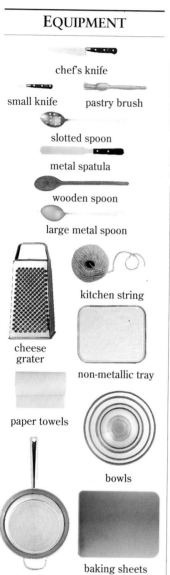

chef's knife

small knife   pastry brush

slotted spoon

metal spatula

wooden spoon

large metal spoon

cheese grater

kitchen string

non-metallic tray

paper towels

bowls

frying pan

baking sheets

9- x 13-inch baking dish   saucepan

chopping board

Thin slices of lightly baked eggplant are wrapped around ricotta and mozzarella cheeses, flavored with basil. Baked in a thick tomato sauce with a sprinkling of Parmesan cheese, they resemble filled pasta cannelloni. Choose broad eggplants that will provide wide slices for filling.

GETTING AHEAD
The "cannelloni" can be baked 2 days ahead. Cover and chill. Reheat 15-20 minutes at 350° F.

* plus 30 minutes standing time

SHOPPING LIST

4	medium eggplants, total weight about 3 lb
	salt and pepper
¼ cup	olive oil
8 oz	mozzarella cheese
1	medium bunch of fresh basil
8 oz	ricotta cheese
¼ cup	grated Parmesan cheese
	For the tomato sauce
3 lb	medium tomatoes
5	garlic cloves
3	medium onions
⅓ cup	olive oil
6 tbsp	tomato paste
1	bouquet garni (see box, page 118)
	sugar

INGREDIENTS

eggplants

bouquet garni   garlic cloves

fresh basil

tomato paste   tomatoes

olive oil   grated Parmesan cheese

sugar

onions

mozzarella cheese   ricotta cheese

ORDER OF WORK

1 PREPARE THE EGGPLANTS

2 MAKE THE TOMATO SAUCE

3 FILL AND BAKE THE EGGPLANT CANNELLONI

1 PREPARE THE EGGPLANTS

1 Trim the eggplants and cut them lengthwise into 3/8-inch slices. Lay the slices on the non-metallic tray, in one layer, and sprinkle them generously on both sides with salt. Leave 30 minutes. Heat the oven to 375°F.

ANNE SAYS
"*Salting eggplant slices draws out the bitter juices.*"

Chef's knife cuts cleanly through eggplant

2 Rinse the eggplant slices with cold water and dry them on paper towels. Lightly brush one side of each slice with olive oil and set slices oil-side down on the baking sheets. Brush the tops with more oil.

Brush on oil lightly because eggplant will absorb it all

3 Bake the eggplant slices until they are tender and lightly browned, turning them once, about 20 minutes. Meanwhile, make the tomato sauce. Let the slices cool on the baking sheets. Leave the oven heated.

! TAKE CARE !
Bake eggplant slices just until tender, otherwise they will be too soft to handle.

2 MAKE THE TOMATO SAUCE

1 Score an "x" on the base of each tomato. Immerse in boiling water until the skin starts to split. Transfer to cold water, then peel. Halve the tomatoes, squeeze out seeds, and chop.

After blanching, skins will slip off easily

2 Strike flat side of the chef's knife on each garlic clove. Peel garlic and finely chop. Peel onions, leaving a little root attached, and cut in half. Slice each half horizontally, leaving attached at root end, then slice vertically, again leaving root end uncut. Cut across to make dice. Chop dice until very fine.

HOW TO MAKE A BOUQUET GARNI

3 Heat the oil in the frying pan, add the diced onions, and cook over medium heat, stirring occasionally with the wooden spoon, until soft but not brown, 3-4 minutes. Add the garlic, tomato paste, bouquet garni, chopped tomatoes, a pinch of sugar, salt and pepper. Cover and cook over very low heat about 10 minutes.

4 Uncover the frying pan and continue cooking the tomato sauce, stirring occasionally, until it is thick, about 15 minutes longer. Lift out the bouquet garni with the wooden spoon and discard it. Taste the sauce for seasoning and adjust if necessary.

This package of flavoring herbs is designed to be easily lifted from the pot and discarded at the end of cooking. To make, hold 2-3 sprigs of fresh thyme, 1 bay leaf, and 10-12 parsley stems together. Wind a piece of string around the herbs and tie, leaving a length to tie to the pot handle if necessary.

3 FILL AND BAKE THE EGGPLANT CANNELLONI

1 Spread about one-third of the tomato sauce in the bottom of the baking dish.

2 Cut the mozzarella into ½-inch slices, and then into ½-inch sticks. Pull the basil leaves from the stems, reserving a few basil sprigs for garnish.

ANNE SAYS
"You will need a basil leaf for each slice of eggplant."

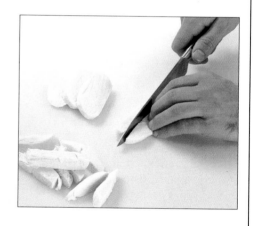

Put mozzarella at narrow end ready to roll up eggplant

3 Using the metal spatula, spread a slice of eggplant with 1 tbsp ricotta cheese. Put a basil leaf at one end, set a mozzarella stick on top, and sprinkle with pepper. Roll up the eggplant slice. Trim the ends of the mozzarella if necessary.

4 Transfer the roll to the baking dish and repeat with the remaining eggplant slices, ricotta, basil, and mozzarella cheese, filling the dish with the "cannelloni."

5 Spoon the remaining tomato sauce over the "cannelloni" and sprinkle with the grated Parmesan cheese. Bake in the oven until very hot and bubbling, 20-25 minutes.

Spoon on tomato sauce to cover cannelloni evenly

🍴 **TO SERVE**
Transfer servings of eggplant "cannelloni" to individual warmed plates, spoon some of the tomato sauce on top, and decorate with the reserved basil sprigs.

Eggplant cannelloni is rich and succulent

EGGPLANT NAPOLEONS

1 Trim the eggplants and cut them crosswise into $3/8$-inch rounds. There should be 36 rounds (6 per person). Spread them on a large non-metallic tray, sprinkle with salt, and leave 20-30 minutes, then rinse, dry, and bake with olive oil as directed.

2 Make the tomato sauce as directed, cooking 5-10 minutes longer to remove extra moisture. Let it cool to tepid.

3 Cut 10 oz mozzarella cheese into 24 $1/4$-inch slices.

4 Stir the ricotta cheese into half of the cooled tomato sauce and taste for seasoning.

5 Pull the basil leaves from the stems, saving 6 sprigs for garnish.

6 Oil a baking sheet. Spread a large eggplant round with about 2-3 tbsp of the tomato and cheese filling, top with a slice of mozzarella and 2-3 basil leaves, then add another round of eggplant, smaller than the first. Repeat with another layer of the filling, cheese, and basil, and finish with a small round of eggplant. Secure the resulting "napoleon" shape with a wooden toothpick so it holds together during baking.

7 Transfer to the baking sheet and continue with the remaining eggplant rounds and filling.

8 Bake the napoleons in the heated oven just until very hot and the mozzarella has melted, 10-15 minutes.

9 Reheat the remaining tomato sauce. Spoon onto warmed individual plates and set the hot napoleons on top. Remove the toothpicks and decorate each serving with a sprig of basil.

SUMMER FRITTATA WITH RATATOUILLE

🍽 SERVES 3-4　🥣 WORK TIME 20-25 MINUTES*　☕ BAKING TIME 20-25 MINUTES

EQUIPMENT

whisk

slotted spoon

chef's knife

fork

small knife

kitchen scissors

string

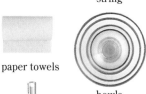
paper towels

bowls

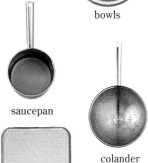
saucepan

colander

tray

10-inch frying pan with lid**

chopping board

**omelet pan can also be used

Frittata is an Italian-style omelet. The flavoring here is a ratatouille of late summer vegetables, but any chopped leftover vegetable you have on hand can be substituted – and while the eggs cook slowly, you can sit back and enjoy a glass of wine.

GETTING AHEAD

The ratatouille filling can be prepared up to 24 hours ahead and refrigerated. Cook the frittata just before serving.

* plus standing and cooling time

SHOPPING LIST

6	eggs
	salt and pepper
1-2 tbsp	butter
	For the ratatouille filling
1	large bouquet garni, made with 10-12 parsley stems, 4-5 fresh thyme sprigs, and 2 bay leaves
1	small eggplant, weighing about 8 oz
1	medium zucchini, weighing about 4 oz
2	garlic cloves
1	medium onion
8 oz	tomatoes
1	medium green bell pepper
5-7	sprigs of fresh thyme
¼ cup	olive oil, more if needed
½ tsp	ground coriander

INGREDIENTS

tomatoes

green bell pepper

onion

butter

olive oil

eggs

zucchini

eggplant

fresh thyme

bouquet garni

ground coriander

garlic cloves

ORDER OF WORK

1 PREPARE THE RATATOUILLE FILLING

2 COOK THE RATATOUILLE FILLING

3 COOK THE FRITTATA

1 PREPARE THE RATATOUILLE FILLING

1 Tie together herbs for bouquet garni with string. Trim the eggplant and cut it lengthwise in half, then cut each half into 4-5 lengthwise strips. Cut the strips across into ³⁄₈-inch chunks.

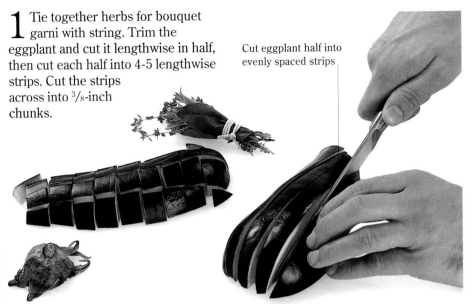

Cut eggplant half into evenly spaced strips

2 Discard the ends from the zucchini and cut it lengthwise in half. Cut each half crosswise into ³⁄₈-inch slices.

3 Put the eggplant and zucchini on the tray and sprinkle generously with salt. Leave 30 minutes to draw out the bitter juices. Transfer to the colander, rinse with cold water and pat dry with paper towels.

6 Cut the cores from the tomatoes and score an "x" on the base of each with the tip of a knife. Immerse them in boiling water until the skin splits, 8-15 seconds depending on their ripeness. Transfer them at once to a bowl of cold water. When cold, peel off the skin.

4 Strike the flat side of the chef's knife on each garlic clove with your fist. Skin and finely chop the cloves.

Use small knife to pull skin from tomatoes

5 Peel the onion, leaving a little of the root attached, and cut it in half through the root and stem. Lay each onion half flat on the chopping board and cut vertically into thin slices.

ANNE SAYS
"The root holds the onion together."

7 Cut the tomatoes crosswise in half, squeeze out the seeds and discard. Chop each half.

8 With a sharp movement, twist the core out of the bell pepper, then halve the pepper and scrape out the seeds. Cut away the white ribs on the inside. Set each pepper half cut-side down on the board and slice it lengthwise into strips.

Lay pepper skin-side up when slicing

9 Strip the thyme leaves from the stems, reserving a few small sprigs for decoration, and pile the leaves on the chopping board. With the chef's knife, finely chop the leaves.

2 COOK THE RATATOUILLE FILLING

1 Heat about half of the oil in the frying pan. Add the eggplant pieces to the pan and stir-fry until browned, 3-5 minutes. Transfer to a bowl with the slotted spoon.

2 Put the zucchini in the pan and stir-fry, adding more oil if necessary, until browned, about 3 minutes. Transfer to the bowl and set aside with the eggplant.

3 Add the green pepper strips to the pan with a little more oil and stir-fry until limp; remove the strips to the bowl. Heat about 1 tbsp more oil in the pan, add the onion, and sauté until lightly browned, 2-3 minutes.

Crisp strips of green pepper will soften as they fry

4 Return the eggplant, zucchini, and green pepper to the pan and add the tomatoes, garlic, salt, pepper, chopped thyme, coriander, and the bouquet garni. Stir until mixed. Cover and cook until all the vegetables are tender, 10-15 minutes. Discard the bouquet garni. Let cool completely.

3 COOK THE FRITTATA

1 Whisk the eggs in a bowl until completely mixed. Stir in the ratatouille mixture and season with salt and pepper.

2 Wipe the frying pan; melt the butter over medium heat until foaming, then add the egg mixture.

3 Reduce the heat, cover with the lid, and cook very gently until the center of the frittata is set, and the base is cooked and lightly browned when you lift the edge with the fork, 20-25 minutes.

Lift edge of frittata gently to check if it is cooked

Fresh thyme sprigs mirror herb flavoring of omelet

!◉! TO SERVE
Invert the frittata onto a large warmed plate and decorate with the reserved thyme sprigs. Cut the frittata into wedges for serving.

CORN, SCALLION, AND RED PEPPER FRITTATA

Yellow corn, green scallions, and red bell peppers make this a colorful and easy alternative to the ratatouille filling.

1 Cook 3 ears of corn in a large pan of boiling water until the kernels pop out easily when tested with the point of a knife, 5-7 minutes. Drain and cut the kernels from the cob. Alternatively, defrost 1½ cups frozen corn kernels.
2 Slice 4 scallions. Core, seed, and slice 1 medium red bell pepper.
3 Peel and dice 2 medium potatoes (total weight about 8 oz). Put them in a pan of water, add salt, bring to a boil, and simmer until tender, 6-8 minutes. Drain thoroughly.
4 Whisk the eggs in a bowl until well mixed and stir in the corn kernels, scallions, red pepper, and potato. Season with salt and pepper.
5 Cook the frittata as directed in the main recipe. Run a knife around the edge of the frittata to loosen it, and slide it onto a warmed plate for serving.

VEGETABLE KNOW-HOW

Thanks to modern methods of extending the shelf life of perishable vegetables, we are offered year-round an astonishing array of both familiar and unusual types. This bounty is the result of modern cultivation, genetic engineering, and improved transportation. Vegetables are often uniform in size, shape, and color, but flavor is sometimes sacrificed to convenience, so local garden produce is worth seeking out when available.

CHOOSING VEGETABLES

It is important to know how to choose vegetables at the market. Each type of vegetable has its own indicator of quality, but generally firmness and bright color are the keys to freshness. Cut stems should be moist and leaves crisp. Young vegetables and dwarf varieties will usually be more tender and sweet, although vegetables that are actually immature often lack juice and may be bitter. Vegetables

VEGETABLES AND YOUR HEALTH

With health concerns on the rise, many cooks turn to vegetables, with their high vitamin and nutrient content, low calories, and lack of cholesterol, to provide the basis for main dishes. Fresh vegetables can come to life with just a dash of lemon juice and a sprinkling of herbs. And other vegetables, such as onions and tomatoes, can be added to enhance flavor and richness. Many of the recipes in **Main Dish Vegetables** are naturally healthy, containing little or no butter, eggs, or heavy cream: Vegetable Couscous and Thai Stir-Fried Vegetables are two examples. And with simple modifications, other vegetable dishes in this book can be made healthier and less fattening.

For frying, butter can be replaced with olive or vegetable oil or with polyunsaturated margarine. You can use polyunsaturated margarine in pastry recipes, too, although they will suffer in taste and texture without some butter content. Omit the piroshki from Borscht and the walnut-garlic sauce from Stuffed Vegetable Trio. With these simple changes, you can enjoy vegetable dishes that are both tempting and light.

grown hydroponically – with their roots in nutrient-rich water instead of soil – look pretty, but their flavor is usually more bland than those grown in soil. Here are specific tips on what to look for when buying vegetables.

Hearty greens, such as *spinach, collards, kale, dandelion greens,* and *sorrel:* young with small tender leaves that are fresh and springy to the touch; no limp, dry, or yellowed leaves and woody stems that show old age. *Cabbage:* crisp leaves and bright color; no brown or damaged patches or discolored veins. Tight-leaved heads of green and red cabbage should be firm and heavy, not puffy. *Brussels sprouts:* small, tightly closed heads and bright green color; no wilted leaves. *Broccoli:* firm stems and closely packed deep green florets. *Cauliflower:* fresh smell and firm head with no brown spots, loose florets, or limp leaves. For both broccoli and cauliflower, size of head is no indication of quality. *Broccoli di rape:* dark green leaves and a strong stem; no wilted leaves or droopy florets. *Tomatoes:* deep color, firm, not soft, and smooth with no splits. *Tomatillos,* sometimes called green tomatoes: firm with pale green skin. *Eggplant:* shiny, firm, and weighty; no brown or soft spots. *Bell peppers:* bright color and firm with no soft spots. *Cucumbers:* firm with no soft spots or blemishes; if puffy they can be too mature with bitter taste and large seeds. *Okra:* no more than 4 inches long with bright green color; skin should puncture crisply when pierced with a fingernail. *Green beans:* bright color, a snappy pod, and no soft spots; if the beans inside are large, the pod will be tough. *Shelling beans,* such as *limas:* plump moist pods with no brown streaks; beans should be small and moist. *Green peas:* plump pods and small deep-green peas; no wrinkles. *Snow* and *sugar snap peas:* crisp and moist. *Corn:* moist green husk with a fresh tassel and no signs of worms; kernels should be unformed at tip but small and tightly packed elsewhere. *Summer squash,* such as *zucchini:* soft, thin, unbroken skin; firm with no soft or brown patches. *Winter squash,* such as *pumpkin:* hard skin with no soft patches; heavy for its size. *Onions* and *shallots:* firm with dry skin; no sign of sprouting. *Scallions* and *leeks:* bright green tops and firm texture; no dry or slimy leaves. *Roots and tubers that grow underground,* including *carrots, turnips, beets, kohlrabi, celery root, Jerusalem artichoke, daikon,* and *jicama:* firm and heavy in the hand, with fresh leaves if the tops are still attached; no flabby damaged flesh and dry patches. Select loose roots in preference to those in packages. *Potatoes:* firm and heavy in the hand; no soft spots, green or black discoloration, or sprouted eyes. *New potatoes* should have skin that rubs away easily with your fingers. *Sweet potatoes* and *yams:* firm with no decaying spots. *Asparagus:* straight and plump, with even-sized stems and tightly budded tips; thick spears are often more tender than thin. *Celery:* light-colored, crisp, and brittle; no brown patches. *Fennel bulbs:* white or light green, crisp, and fully formed; no brown patches. *Swiss chard:* firm white stalks and fresh unwilted dark green leaves. Mediterranean *cardoon:* dark green leaves and silver-gray, supple stalks with a small root. *Globe artichokes:* compact green heads with no dark patches or dry streaks; on most varieties the leaves spread when too mature. Diameter of base, not size of artichoke, indicates size of bottom. *Button mushrooms:* moist, white, or light tan caps with no discoloration; stems should not be dry. *Wild mushrooms: shiitake* should be moist and fleshy; *oyster mushrooms* should have soft silky caps and no dark wet patches; *chanterelles* should have large moist trumpets of deep color and stem ends that are not dry; *morels* should have a fragrant smell and clean caps that are not dry. *Salad greens:* all should have a fresh smell and crisp green leaves. *Belgian endive:* crisp pale heads; *chicory* family: heavy heads with a pale heart; *butterhead* and *Boston lettuce:* soft leaves with a well-formed heart; *radicchio:* well-formed heart; *arugula:* long leaves; *mâche:* soft green leaves; *cress:* crunchy green leaves with no yellowing.

STORING VEGETABLES

The type of vegetable and how ripe it is when you buy it determine how long it can be kept. Root vegetables and hardy winter squashes keep well at cool room temperature (around 60°F). Trim the tops off root vegetables, such as carrots and beets, to prevent juices flowing to the leaves, leaving the root dry. Store greens and soft vegetables, such as cucumbers, in the refrigerator on the lower shelves or in the crisper compartment, loosely folded in a cloth. Do not use airtight wrapping such as a plastic bag because this encourages rotting and bacteria. Different vegetables are best stored separately and away from fruit, which emits a gas that makes carrots bitter, for example. Onions cause potatoes to spoil more quickly and taint dairy products.

PREPARING VEGETABLES

Do not wash vegetables until just before you use them because moisture encourages rot and extracts vitamins. Vegetables that absorb water easily, such as potatoes, are often boiled or steamed with the skin left on so that they retain their vitamins and absorb less moisture. Beets will not bleed if cooked with their skin. Vegetables that are waxed, as is often the case with cucumbers, should be peeled

HOW-TO BOXES

There are pictures of all preparation steps for each **Main Dish Vegetables** *recipe. Some basic techniques are general to a number of recipes; they are shown in extra detail in these special "how-to" boxes.*

before using. Before peeling bell peppers they are charred under the broiler to loosen their skins, and tomatoes are blanched. Some vegetables, such as eggplant, may be baked and the cooked flesh scooped out of the skin. Many modern pesticides are concentrated in vegetable skin and cannot be removed simply by washing in water. Peeling vegetables therefore reduces the likelihood of contamination.

Some vegetables, such as artichoke bottoms and celery root, discolor easily when cut. Use a stainless steel knife to prevent discoloration from carbon steel, and drop the prepared vegetables immediately into water acidulated with lemon juice, until ready to cook them.

INDEX

ACKNOWLEDGMENTS

Photographers David Murray
Jules Selmes
Photographer's Assistant Ian Boddy

Chef Eric Treuille
Cookery Consultant Linda Collister
Assisted by Joanna Pitchfork

US Editor Jeanette Mall

Typesetting Rowena Feeny
Assisted by Robert Moore
Text film by Disc to Print (UK) Limited

Production Consultant Lorraine Baird

*Anne Willan would like to thank
her chief editor Cynthia Nims and
associate editor Kate Krader for their
vital help with writing the book and
researching and testing the recipes, aided
by Randall Price and La Varenne's
chefs and trainees.*